# Dispositions

*We dedicate this book to our children, grandchildren, and great-grandchildren, who will be living throughout the 21st century and well into the 22nd century. If the concepts in this book become fully implemented, they will grow up in an increasingly empathic, compassionate, peaceful, and thought-full world.*

# Dispositions

*Reframing Teaching and Learning*

## Arthur L. Costa

*Professor Emeritus,*
*California State University, Sacramento,*
*Cofounder, Institute for Habits of Mind*

## Bena Kallick

*Program Director, Eduplanet21,*
*Cofounder, Institute for Habits of Mind*

*Foreword by Yong Zhao*

**CORWIN**
A SAGE Company

**CORWIN**
A SAGE Company

FOR INFORMATION:

Corwin

A SAGE Company

2455 Teller Road

Thousand Oaks, California 91320

(800) 233-9936

www.corwin.com

SAGE Publications Ltd.

1 Oliver's Yard

55 City Road

London EC1Y 1SP

United Kingdom

SAGE Publications India Pvt. Ltd.

B 1/I 1 Mohan Cooperative Industrial Area

Mathura Road, New Delhi 110 044

India

SAGE Publications Asia-Pacific Pte. Ltd.

3 Church Street

#10-04 Samsung Hub

Singapore 049483

Copyright © 2014 by Corwin

Printed in the United States of America

*Cataloging-in-publication data is available from the Library of Congress.*

ISBN 978-1-4833-3910-8

This book is printed on acid-free paper.

Acquisitions Editor:   Dan Alpert

Associate Editor:   Kimberly Greenberg

Production Editor:   Olivia Weber-Stenis

Copy Editor:   Codi Bowman

Typesetter:   C&M Digitals (P) Ltd.

Proofreader:   Pam Suwinsky

Indexer:   Molly Hall

Cover Designer:   Michael Dubowe

Marketing Manager:   Stephanie Trkay

13 14 15 16 17 10 9 8 7 6 5 4 3 2 1

# Contents

# Foreword

*By Yong Zhao*

"**I**s Google making us stupid?" asked Nicholas Carr, author of *The Big Switch: Rewiring the World, From Edison to Google*, in a 2008 *Atlantic* article.[1] Carr was lamenting the loss of the habit and even ability of deep reading due to the arrival of the Internet. "The deep reading that used to come naturally has become a struggle," wrote Carr, "And what the Net seems to be doing is chipping away my capacity for concentration and contemplation."

Carr's chief problem with the Net is the style of reading it seems to engender, "a style that puts 'efficiency' and 'immediacy' above all else." "When we read online," wrote Carr, referencing Maryanne Wolf, a developmental psychologist at Tufts University, "we tend to become 'mere decoders of information.' Our ability to interpret text, to make the rich mental connections that form when we read deeply and without distraction, remains largely disengaged."

What Carr has me worried about the impact of Google is what Arthur L. Costa and Bena Kallick have me worried about teaching in our schools. Driven by standardized testing that aims to assess our children's ability to provide prescribed answers, the education our children receive in schools may be making them stupid.

"Our practices of assessment, now and planned for the future, focus on the student's ability to provide correct answers," write Costa and Kallick. "Teachers report that such testing has an impact on their teaching." As a result, "they tend to spend more time covering material in class that will appear on standardized tests."

---

[1] http://www.theatlantic.com/magazine/archive/2008/07/is-google-making-us-stupid/306868/

Standardized testing has been used as the primary driver for education reform in the United States over the past few decades. Test scores—that is, student ability to give the answers deemed correct by authorities—have been equated with the ability to live a successful life and hence should be pursued at any cost by students, teachers, and schools.

Costa and Kallick make it apparent that success is not defined by test scores. Rather, it is better defined by the attitudes and dispositions that learners bring to any new knowledge. And they make it immediately apparent that these dispositions are what teachers around the world want to see their students demonstrating.

With the imminent implementation of the Common Core State Standards Initiative, millions of children in the United States will not only be held accountable for finding answers to standardized tests, but also standardized tests of only two sets of knowledge and skills prescribed by a group of "content experts." They are expected to be able to find the expected answers at the expected time in the expected format—because the Common Core wants common assessment and prescribes common grade-level expectations.

Given past experiences with high-stakes testing, it is to be expected that the Common Core will further transform education into test preparation rather than focusing on the important 21st-century skills that so many proclaim are essential in order to be prepared for college and career. It seems unavoidable that teachers, school leaders, students, and even parents will narrow children's educational experiences to activities that help children achieve good test scores as the stakes grow even higher for all parties involved. And the stakes are getting higher. The Partnership for Assessment of Readiness for College and Careers (PARCC), one of the two Common Assessment consortia, for example, promises that its College and Career Readiness Determination:

- Will provide policymakers, educators, parents, and students with a clear signal about the level of academic preparation needed for success in these postsecondary courses.
- Will provide a strong indicator of college and career readiness that can be used to set performance goals at any level and show progress towards those goals.

- Finally, students who attain a CCR Determination in ELA/ literacy and/or mathematics will have a tangible benefit – direct entry into relevant entry-level, credit-bearing courses without need for remediation.[2]

According to Carr, Google seeks to develop the "perfect search engine that understands exactly what you mean and gives you back exactly what you want." It sounds like what standardized tests want—students who understand exactly what the test makers mean and give back exactly what they want. Thus, preparing students to find answers on standardized tests is much like developing "intelligent" information processing machines, the perfect search engine. In other words, we are turning the nation's schools into little Google offices to create millions of much less efficient Google search engines.

But "a perfect search engine" is not what will make children successful in life because intelligence is much more than collecting, storing, analyzing, and spitting out information. Even PARCC acknowledges the limitation of the Common Core:

> It must be noted that the academic knowledge, skills, and practices defined by the PARCC CCR Determinations in ELA/ literacy and mathematics are an essential part of students' readiness for college and careers, but do not encompass the full range of knowledge, skills, and practices students need for success in postsecondary programs and careers. For example, Conley (2012) includes learning skills and techniques such as persistence, motivation, and time management as critical elements of college and career readiness, along with transition skills and knowledge such as awareness of postsecondary norms and culture and career awareness.

Thus education should not just be about information processing. What distinguish human beings from machines are emotions, intuition, and individual diversity. Education must include the development of the human elements in our children. Costa

---

[2]http://www.parcconline.org/sites/parcc/files/PARCCCCRDPolicyandPLDs_ FINAL_0.pdf

and Kallick present a reasonable, practical, and positive alternative—the cultivation of dispositional thinking, the very core of being human. They develop a compelling case for reframing and re-aligning instruction and assessment with 21st-century goals. They provide ample lists of dispositions from which to build a functional curriculum. They offer an intriguing strategy for assessment which involves students in describing the behaviors they see themselves using if they are performing the dispositions. More importantly, the locus of evaluation from others shifts to students becoming more self-managing, self-monitoring and self-modifying—truly the goals of self-directed education. The dispositions thereby become internalized.

Moreover, dispositions provide an excellent guide for teachers, parents, and everyone who cares about education to develop schools and communities as cultures of dispositional thinking. This book is a powerful antidote to the increasing mechanization of education and should be read by all who care to move education beyond search engine development. After all, education should not make us stupid.

Yong Zhao
University of Oregon
Eugene, Oregon

# Acknowledgments

The thoughts, concepts, and ideas contained in this book are the product of our learning from and with many great minds and thinkers in the fields of cognition, intellectual development, education, and psychology. We have had great teachers:

Guy Claxton, Centre for Real-World Learning, Winchester University, England

Reuven Feuerstein, International Center for the Enhancement of Learning Potential, Jerusalem, Israel

Robert Garmston, Professor Emeritus, California State University, Sacramento

Heidi Hayes Jacobs, President, Curriculum Designers, Rye, NY

Jay Mctighe, President, Jay Mctighe & Associates, MD

David Perkins, Project Zero, Harvard University, Cambridge, MA

Ron Ritchhart, Project Zero, Harvard University, Cambridge, MA

Shari Tishman, Project Zero, Harvard University, Cambridge, MA

Grant Wiggins, President, Authentic Education, Hopewell, NJ

Pat Wolfe, Mind Matters, Inc., Napa, California

Some of our most powerful learning has come from the many students, teachers, and administrators in schools around the world who have embraced these ideas, implemented them, and celebrated the results. They have given us the courage and impetus to spread the word so that others may benefit.

# About the Authors

**Arthur L. Costa, EdD,** is an emeritus professor of Education at California State University, Sacramento. He is cofounder of the Institute for Habits of Mind and cofounder of the Center for Cognitive Coaching. He served as a classroom teacher, a curriculum consultant, and an assistant superintendent for instruction in the Office of the Sacramento County Superintendent of Schools and as the director of educational programs for the National Aeronautics and Space Administration. He has made presentations and conducted workshops in all 50 states as well as on six of the seven continents.

Active in many professional organizations, Art served as president of the California Association for Supervision and Curriculum Development and was the National President of Association for Supervision and Curriculum Development from 1988 to 1989. He was the recipient of the prestigious Lifetime Achievement Award from the National Urban Alliance in 2010.

**Bena Kallick, PhD,** is a private consultant providing services to school districts, state departments of education, professional organizations, and public agencies throughout the United States and abroad. Kallick received her doctorate in educational evaluation at Union Graduate School. Her areas of focus include group dynamics, creative and critical thinking, and alternative assessment strategies for the classroom. Formerly a Teachers' Center director, Kallick also created a children's museum based on problem solving and invention. She was the coordinator of a high school alternative designed for at-risk students. She is cofounder of Performance Pathways, a company dedicated to providing easy-to-use software for curriculum mapping and assessment tracking and reporting, an integrated suite. She was a strategic adviser for SunGard Public Sector K–12 on behalf of Performance Plus, a transformational new product based on the work of Performance Pathways. She is known for her practical approach to making curriculum mapping and assessment a catalyst for improving teaching and learning.

Kallick's teaching appointments have included Yale University School of Organization and Management, University of Massachusetts Center for Creative and Critical Thinking, and Union Graduate School. She was formerly on the board of the Apple Foundation, the board of Jobs for the Future and Weston Woods Institute. She presently serves on the board of Communities for Learning.

Her work with Dr. Art Costa has led to the development of the Institute for Habits of Mind (www.instituteforhabitsofmind.com), an international institute that is dedicated to transforming schools into places where thinking and habits of mind are taught, practiced, valued, and have become infused into the culture of the school and community. The institute provides services and products to support bringing the habits of mind into the culture of schools and the communities they serve.

She and Art Costa have just completed an online course for Eduplanet21, a company that is dedicated to professional development for educators using the most contemporary tools and thinking to be successful engaging students as 21st-century learners. In addition, she is the program director for this company.

CHAPTER ONE

# Introduction

## Challenging the Mindset

"**M**ind the gap!" The plane parked at the Jetway at London's Heathrow Airport. The engines shut down. "Welcome to the United Kingdom," greeted the flight attendant. "Take caution when you exit the plane. There is a gap between the level of the jet bridge and the floor of the plane. Don't get your shoe caught. Mind the gap!" The flight attendant was calling our attention to the difference in levels between the floor of the plane and the Jetway.

This story is a good metaphor for the purpose of this book, which calls attention to the gap between what we claim that we value as 21st-century educational essentials and what we value in our assessments of teachers, students, schools, and even nation's educational systems. As we examine the many lists of desired learnings to prepare our future citizens for a life of problem solving, uncertainty, and globalization, and given the access we have to information through technologies, it becomes apparent that the keys to learning are dispositional in nature. Intended in this discussion, and for our purposes, when we say dispositions, we are referring to thinking dispositions—tendencies toward particular patterns of intellectual behavior.

Our practices of assessment, however, now and planned for the future, focus on the student's ability to provide correct answers (Dean, 2010). Teachers report that such testing has an impact on their teaching. Unfortunately, they tend to spend

1

more time covering material in class that will appear on standardized tests and worry that they won't cover everything before the tests are administered (Ferriter, 2013). These types of measures are no longer sufficient. If students are to achieve their full potential, they must have opportunities to engage, develop, and demonstrate a much richer set of skills and dispositions (U.S. Department of Education, 2013, p. v). This book calls attention to this gap.

We need to align our curriculum with the stated needs of students in their future lives. This book is intended to raise awareness of the need for dispositional teaching and learning, to provide rationale for transforming our educational system to value and to assess growth in dispositional learning as valid educational outcomes.

We are not suggesting that we abandon nor should we diminish the teaching of basic skills and knowledge of significant, relevant content and conceptual understandings. These, too, are essential for our students' future. Dispositions not only direct our strategic abilities, they also help activate relevant content knowledge as well, bringing that knowledge to the forefront to better illuminate the situation at hand (Ritchhart, 2002). Thinking dispositions develop resourcefulness (capacities) for expanding that knowledge and those skills and capabilities. Dispositional thinking informs and mediates that knowledge and those skills and capabilities (Feuerstein, Feuerstein, & Falik, 2010, p. xviii). Intelligent action in the world is what counts most. Knowledge of content is only a part of performance. Of equal importance is becoming alert to occasions for the application and the inclination to put skills and knowledge into play. Dispositions become the patterns of a student's exhibited behavior over time (Davidson, 2013).

Furthermore, the processes of acquiring content knowledge have changed drastically because of technology. Ask students to compare ancient Egypt with Mesopotamia, for example, and their first move is to the computer to "Ask Jeeves," query Wikipedia, search Google Scholar, or enlist a response to the question on a social network. (To search the Web well, however, requires the dispositions of flexibility, persistence, and the use of clear and precise language [O'Hanlon, 2013].) We are suggesting, however, that if we believe that 21st-century dispositions are also essential, that they, too, become the subject of curriculum, instruction, student assessment, and even teacher evaluation. We will need to reframe our assessment of successful students, which in turn influences how we assess successful teachers and even successful schools (Costa, Garmston, & Zimmerman, 2014). Might we give equal attention to students' reading skills as well as their love of reading; their knowledge of scientific principles as well as their curiosity, intrigue, and wonderment about scientific phenomena; their knowledge and application of mathematical processes as well as their persistence with complex problems? Might we teach not only "right" answers, but also teach our students how to behave when they are confronted with problems the answers to which are elusive. Both are essential. We suggest that well-chosen, intriguing, rich, relevant content serves as a vehicle for experiencing the "joyride" of learning. The focus is not only learning *of* the content but also learning *from* the content.

We draw on our 20-plus years of experience implementing skillful thinking, self-directed learning, and the Habits of Mind—one subset of dispositions—in schools and classrooms around the world. We've learned a great deal about teaching students to become more effective thinkers, what works and what doesn't. We've researched and reported on the positive effects of these efforts and, therefore, have a burning desire to spread dispositional teaching and learning to an even greater number of schools and classrooms.

We've worked to define what it means to be an efficacious thinker—the efficacious thinker is not only skillful, but also motivated to employ skillful thinking (Swartz et al., 2007). Knowing the benefits of effective thinking, they are alert to situational cues that signal when it counts; they are conscious of their mental energies and problem-solving strategies; they know when it is appropriate to use skillful thinking, and they reflect on and continually strive to improve their cognitive processes. Being "good" thinkers means they are not only skillful but they are also inclined, disposed, and compelled to employ good thinking.

We've also worked with schools that wished to embrace dispositions—to become "Homes for the Mind" (Costa, 2004). We have learned that it takes time, a shared vision of the staff, and a commitment to building a school culture in which dispositions are the norm—the way we do things around here. We have found that it is much more likely that students will internalize and continue to grow the dispositions if they are consistently and often taught, modeled, reflected on, and reinforced by the entire school community. This is consistent with studies of the brain that show a correlation between frequency and duration of practice and the amount and extent of activity and density of connections (dendrites and synapses) and myelinization in the brain (Willis, 2013). We refer to this frequency of encounters as "Dispositional Density."

The three essential questions that will guide the work of this book are the following:

1. *How do we make dispositions come alive in the minds of students?* Once you've named them, the question is how to give them meaning, build capacities, sensitize students to situations, give them strategies, help them see the value, build commitment to improvement, and move to action that circles back to assessment.

2. *How do we produce a paradigm shift in the thinking of educational leaders, parents, the public, and our political decision makers?* We've learned that to change educational practices there must be a corresponding change in thinking, beliefs, values, and perceptions.

3. *How do we reclaim the role that education must play in protecting our democracy?* The many debates about what is right in education are most often defined by what is good for the economy. This debate becomes polarizing rather than seeking the common good. Thomas Jefferson put this standard forward clearly in stating that the way to protect democracy is by having an educated citizenship. We seek to define how education lives up to that task in the 21st century.

Minding the gap means paying attention to our intentions, aligning theory and practice, and constantly monitoring for congruity. This will require a reframing of our mental maps about what education is for, what are the attributes of "intelligent" human beings, and what needs to go on in schools and classrooms that are dispositionally oriented. It will require a new language with which we communicate about educational purposes, assessments of student progress, and excellence in teaching and learning. We hope this book will help. *Mind the gap!*

# REFERENCES

Costa, A. (2004). *The school as a home for the mind.* Thousand Oaks, CA: Corwin.

Costa, A., Garmston, R., & Zimmerman, D. (2014). *Cognitive capital: Investing in teacher quality.* New York, NY: Teachers College Press.

Davidson, C. N. (2013). *Now you see it: How the brain science of attention will transform the way we live, work, and learn.* New York, NY: Viking Press.

Dean, S. (2010). Preparing to implement next generation assessments. *Blueprint for Educational Leadership. 5, 7.* Retrieved from, http://www.hunt-institute.org/elements/media/files/Blueprint-Number-5

Ferriter, W. (2013). How testing will change what I teach next year. *Center for Teaching Quality.* Retrieved from, www.teachingquality.org/content/how-testing-will-change-what-i-teach-next-year#.UYsiNuD56CN

Feuerstein, R., Feuerstein, R., & Falik, L. (2010). *Beyond smarter: Mediated learning and the brain's capacity for change.* New York, NY: Teachers College Press.

O'Hanlon, L. H. (2013). Teaching students better online research skills: Improving Web research tactics is a priority. *Education Week.* Retrieved from, http://www.edweek.org/ew/articles/2013/05/22/32el-studentresearch.h32.html?tkn=QWCCgXpStXBSdGy%2BRabLBT9BSWvJPFfQ47w2&cmp=clp-sb-ascd

Ritchhart, R. (2002). *Intellectual character: What it is, why it matters, and how to get it.* San Francisco, CA: Jossey Bass.

Swartz, R., et al. (2007). *Thinking based learning.* New York, NY: Teachers College Press.

U.S. Department of Education. Office of Educational Technology. (2013). *Promoting grit, tenacity, and perseverance: Critical factors of success in the 21st Century.* Washington, D. C.: Author.

Willis, J. (2013). Cooperative learning: Accessing our highest human potential. In Costa, A. and O'Leary, P. (Eds.), *The power of the social brain: Teaching learning and interdependent thinking* (pp. 119–128). New York, NY: Teachers College Press.

CHAPTER TWO

# Why Dispositions?

*We don't teach the most important skills: persistence, self-control, curiosity, conscientiousness, grit and self-confidence.*

—Paul Tough (2012)

We need to prepare our students for both the present and a vastly different future than what exists today. With better health care, it is very likely that today's kindergartners will be living well into the 22nd century. There is a confluence of thought and research suggesting that our inventions and innovations are continuously changing our world. Numerous international authoritative futurists, neuroscientists, educators, and sociologists make reference to the need for problem solving, creating, innovating, and communicating to sustain the democratic society in which we live. Although these authors use different terms, they share much in common: The needs they list are *dispositions* that are necessary to lend oneself to learning. In the absence of these dispositions, students are not able to become the productive, innovative problem solvers for our economy and for our democracy. If this is the case, then how are we developing curriculum, designing instruction, and gathering assessment data about students acquiring these dispositions? In this chapter, we make the case for dispositional learning as essential for citizens of the future.

## ADVOCATING DISPOSITIONS

Drawing on Paul Tough's (2012) book for example, the U.S. Department of Education (2013) advocates grit, tenacity, and perseverance as critical factors for success in the 21st century. Pink (2009) refers to the keys to internal motivation as autonomy, mastery, and purpose. Harvard University's Tony Wagner (2008) calls for seven essentials for all our youth: (Visit http://www.youtube.com/watch?v=D3gpjjIOqHA)

1. Problem solving and critical thinking
2. Collaboration across networks and leading by influence
3. Agility and adaptability
4. Initiative and entrepreneurship
5. Effective written and oral communication
6. Accessing and analyzing information
7. Curiosity and imagination

Advocating for college and career readiness, David Conley (2010) refers to a set of key cognitive strategies that enable students to apply what they know and what they are learning in complex ways, as well as develop the ability to manage themselves (e.g., goal setting, time management, being persistent, etc.). He identifies such dispositions as the following:

- Open-mindedness
- Inquisitiveness
- Analyzing the credibility and relevance of sources
- Reasoning, argumentation, and explaining proof and point of view
- Comparing, contrasting ideas, analyzing, and interpreting competing or conflicting evidence
- Knowing how to arrive at an accurate answer
- Finding many ways to solve problems

Thomas Friedman (2012, p. 1) predicts that given the pace of change today, our kids will have to invent a job. They will have to reinvent, reengineer, and reimagine that job much more often than their parents if they want to advance in it. Michael Roth (2012), president of Wesleyan College, in his article, "Learning as Freedom," calls specifically for Habits of Mind, as does Dr. Kim, former president of Dartmouth College and presently CEO of the World Bank. Research in neuroscience, reported in Paul Tough's book *How Children Succeed* (2012), suggests a strong relationship between children's capacity to succeed in learning and the ability to persist, to manage impulsivity, and to communicate—even when their lives are so damaged through poverty and neglect that the will for school work is limited.

Furthermore, we are living in an era of increasing uncertainty, complexity, and ambiguity in which we are bombarded with conflicting models of what to value, what to believe, how to decide, and how to live. As educators, we observe the symptoms of the stress that these uncertainties and confusions produce in school—escapism, bullying, obesity, recklessness, drug abuse, anxiety, depression, self-doubt, violence, and suicide. It is the role of education, as an instrument of American society, to help develop the mental and emotional resources that young people need to cope with the demands of their lives, now and in their future: resilience, efficacy, self-regulation, flexibility, confidence, positivity, self-reliance, interdependence, and, yes, even a sense of humor. Those resources are psychological as much as they are material or social (Lucas, Claxton, & Spencer, 2013).

This attention to dispositions is not only being seen in the United States. At this time in history there is an international surge—an intellectual spring—brought on by the realization that a country's future in the 21st century and beyond depends on its people's—children's and adults'—creativity, problem solving, communication, and collaboration. (For more information on 21st-century skills, see Appendix C.)

Ministries of education in many nations around the world are adopting dispositional teaching and learning. They address the significant knowledge, concepts, and dispositions needed to understand and act creatively and innovatively on issues of global significance. Those competencies and the dispositions they require include such essentials as the following:

- Investigating the world beyond their immediate environment
- Recognizing their and others' perspectives
- Communicating their ideas effectively with diverse audiences

- Translating their ideas and findings into appropriate actions to improve conditions
- These essentials require certain propensities, inclinations or tendencies such as being curious, wondering, questioning, and problem posing
- Taking risks, persisting, striving for accuracy
- Empathizing with others, collaborating, inhibiting impulse, and listening
- Thinking flexibly, communicating with clarity both orally and in writing
- Our democratic way of life demands self-respect and respect for others (Mansilla & Jackson, 2011)

## DISTILLING THE LISTS

Reviewing these lists from the eminent authorities, leaders, and futurists, some connections, patterns, and similarities soon become obvious:

*Dispositional in nature*—Attitudes or inclinations that describe the likelihood, not the certainty, that effective actions will be taken when confronted with problematic situations.

*Cognitive*—These propensities are what goes on in the mind. They are thinking dispositions; they are what might be called mental habits or Habits of Mind.

*Broad, panoramic, and expansive*—Dispositions are intended to describe life skills, attitudes, and behaviors that will be used well beyond the specifics of schooling. There are also some elements that are obvious by their absence from these lists.

- *Operational definitions*—what it looks like, sounds like, or feels like to perform these dispositions
- *Academic knowledge*—for example, knowing mathematical operations or algorithms, understanding scientific vocabulary, laws and principles, knowledge of historical facts and eras, etc.
- *Impact of technology*—attention to how technology affects how and what people learn
- *Aesthetics*—as in the arts, literature, music, or drama
- *Instructional strategies*—cues and directions for how to instill such dispositions in students or others

- *Assessment*—strategies for monitoring growth or increased skillfulness in the performance of these dispositions over time
- *Directions*—for how humans perform them spontaneously without prompting
- *Clues*—as to how the dispositions become "interiorized" in the mind of the learner so as to proactively guide their decisions and actions
- *Affect*—reference to the affective—habits of the heart (See Chapter 9)

## SOFT SKILLS?

These dispositions are often referred to as "noncognitive," and "soft skills" (Conley, 2013; U.S. Department of Education, 2013). To distinguish how students approach different aspects of the learning process, researchers coined the somewhat awkward term "noncognitive" to distinguish attitudes, beliefs, and attributes from content knowledge, which they labeled "cognitive"—everything that was not, in their view, grounded in or directly derived from rational thought. This distinction reflected the idea that one type of thinking formed the basis of knowing and recalling information, and that the other originated in beliefs, attitudes, and feelings. "Soft skills" also sounds as if they are unassessable. A score cannot be derived from counting their use or correctness. There are no right answers, no "hard" data. Thus, their assessment must yield "soft" data.

We disagree with this terminology because we perceive these dispositions as highly cognitive indeed. When confronted with problematic situations, these dispositions serve as an internal compass. Mindful human beings use their executive processes to mindfully, metacognitively employ one or more of these dispositions by asking themselves, "*What is the most thought-full thing I can do right now?*"

Following that question, which sets the stage for a greater awareness of the need to slow down the response to action, some of the following questions might arise, depending on the situation.

*Drawing from past knowledge and applying it to new situations*, one might ask: What are my resources and how can I draw on my past successes with problems like this? What do I already know about this sort of problem? What resources do I have available or need to generate?

**Figure 2.1** What can I do when I don't know the answer immediately?

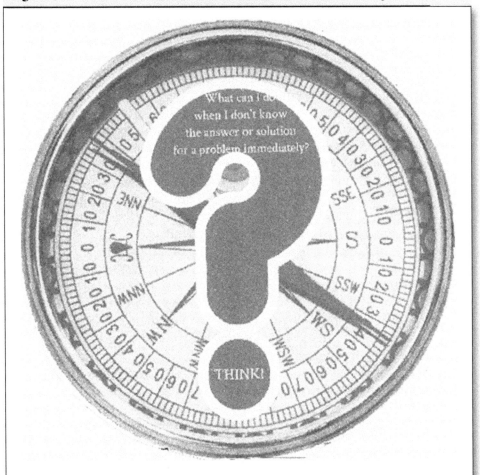

How might I approach this problem *flexibly?* How might I look at the situation in another way, how can I draw on my repertoire of problem-solving strategies, or how can I look at this problem from a fresh perspective (lateral thinking)?

*Striving for precision and accuracy,* one might ask, how might I illuminate this problem to make it clearer, more precise? Do I need to check out my data sources? How might I break this problem down into its component parts and develop a strategy for understanding and accomplishing each step?

*Metacognitively,* one might ask, what do I know or not know? What questions do I need to ask, what strategies are in my mind now, what am I aware of in terms of my beliefs, values, and goals with this problem? What feelings or emotions am I aware of that might be blocking or enhancing my progress?

The *interdependent* thinker might turn to others for help. They might ask how this problem affects others; how can we solve it together, and what can I learn from others that would help me become a better problem solver?

As is evident from these questions, they are anything but "soft." Rather, they are robust, firm, sturdy, and strong. They are even more challenging than such cognitive skills as recalling and understanding information because they require self-awareness, inhibition of impulse, and management of internal thought processes, being alert to situational cues, skillfully employing capacities, and gathering feedback about results. Learning these dispositions takes time, practice, self-monitoring, and reflection.


## MIND THE GAP

It is also interesting and revealing to compare these lists with what actually goes on in most schools and classrooms today. Few would argue with the statements in the lists. In fact, they are the words and phrases that populate many schools' mission and vision statements. Here is a typical example:

> City High School is a home for the active mind—a cooperative community promoting knowledge, self-understanding, mutual respect, global understanding, adaptability to change, and a love for lifelong learning.

Argyris and Schön (1974) distinguish between espoused theory and theory-in-use. They assert that people hold maps in their heads about how to plan, implement, and review their actions. Few people, however, are aware that the maps they use to take action are not the theories they explicitly espouse.

Like the baseball player who has a vision of himself hitting a home run but has no idea how to do it, there's a gap. On the one hand, through our curriculum documents, vision statements, and missions, we espouse the teaching of mindfulness, 21st-century dispositions, attitudes, inclinations, and outcomes that are supposed to equip our future generations with the capacities for solving ambiguous, complex global problems. On the other hand, applying the theory-in-use, our schools are governed by a one-size-fits-all common core curriculum, testing that awards right answers and compartmentalized curriculum.

A recent Gallup Poll (Gallup Inc., 2013) discovered that only 28% of high school graduates had the opportunity to work on a project that took several classes to complete, and 22% reported that they were able to develop solutions to real problems in their community or world. This suggests that students may be encouraged to persist, for example, but the nature of the tasks that they are required to do may not reflect persistence based on actual engagement in learning. Rather, there seems to be a curriculum that is designed more for compliance than for the development of curiosity. As long as schools are judged by how well their students perform on content-oriented assessments, valuing dispositions is placed in the background. Teachers are evaluated using inter-rater reliable rubrics. Therein lies the gap. Lauren Resnick (1999) suggests that the educational methods we have been using for the past 70 years no longer suffice because they are based on archaic scientific assumptions about the nature of knowledge, the learning process, and differential aptitudes for learning that have been eclipsed by new discoveries.

A good example of this gap is with the current emphasis in the United States on the Common Core State Standards. Forty-five states and the District of Columbia have adopted these standards that set a framework for what concepts and skills should be mastered in math and English language arts in K–12 education. The National Science Teachers Association and the National Research Council have released a set of K–12 science standards that similarly stress acquiring a deep understanding of concepts through analytical scientific inquiry.

These standards call for more rigor, complex reasoning, problem solving, and critical thinking than traditional learning. Much effort is being expended by publishers, e-book developers, curriculum designers, staff developers, and product designers to revise and align curriculum; train teachers in how to engage students with greater rigor, complexity, abstract reasoning; and to develop strategies that will assess students' deepened understanding and ability to find relationships, connections, and patterns among diverse sources. The tests being developed to measure students' achievement of these standards often yield scores based on "right" answers.

We believe, however, that school subjects such as math, science, social sciences, and literacy provide not only desirable conceptual understandings, they provide opportunities with which students experience wonderment, intrigue, and a desire for life-long learning. Along with such standards and expectations, we must also focus on those bigger outcomes—the long-term transfer goals and the qualities of mind—that it's hoped the study of such school subjects promotes. Assessments should illuminate growth in the qualities of mind or dispositions that the subjects produce, as well as the content of the discipline.

What was significant and hard to measure has been replaced by what is educationally insignificant and easy to measure. So now we measure how well we taught what isn't worth learning.

This book is about alignment—aligning day-to-day classroom practices with larger, dispositional outcomes. Because this is an adaptive shift, which requires a change of paradigm or mental model, rather than a technical shift such as installing new computers, changing time schedules, or adopting new textbooks, this alignment will require educators, parents, and politicians to think and talk differently about the goals of education. This will necessitate transforming the educational process from a content-oriented, subject-centered, test-driven frame to a view of education being dispositional in nature. We will describe how to design curriculum and teach for and assess growth in dispositional learning.

We offer a choice: One is to continue what we are currently doing in education. Remember, however, that Einstein said, "Insanity is continuing to do the same thing over and over and expecting different results." Another choice is to adopt a new premise—a new view of what schooling is for. Ron Ritchhart (2002) challenges us to think differently:

> What if education were less about acquiring skills and knowledge and more about cultivating the dispositions and habits of mind that students will need for a lifetime of learning, problem-solving and decision-making? What if education were less concerned with the end-of-year-exam and more concerned with who students become as a result of their schooling? What if we viewed smartness as a goal that students can work toward rather than as something they either have or don't? (p. xxii)

School is the place where we all come together. For many students, it is an escape from a chaotic, frequently violent and certainly confusing environment. We cannot continue to allow the work of school to be defined by the political forces that polarize our society. Rather, we must offer our students a social fabric that weaves a story of community, hope, and courage. In the absence of a dedication to these purposes, we will educate technologically but we will not educate the heart. The dispositions are central to our learning to live together in the presence of the content that we teach. The Latin word *educare* means to draw out. Using that definition, here is what we must draw out:

- The strengths and gifts of every student and teacher so that they can make a powerful contribution to the learning community
- The strengths and gifts of our neighborhoods and larger communities so that they can contribute to the students in their quest for a future
- The capacity to debate, dialogue, and harmonize around important ideas by learning how to find our commonalities as well as accepting our differences
- The accountability for education that includes documenting the development of dispositions that serve as a compass for living and working for the common good
- Capacities that students can work toward rather than something they either have or don't

## SUMMARY

As professional educators, we may be pressured for immediate, measurable results on standards-based performances. This assumes that if teachers taught academic subjects and if students were to learn and be evaluated on how well they learn the concepts and subskills in each content area, they will somehow become the kind of people we want them to be (Seiger-Eherenberg, 1991, p. 6). Our desire is to make curriculum, instruction, and assessments more balanced so that students have the opportunity to learn, practice, and demonstrate the development of dispositions. We want our children to develop those dispositions that lead them to become lifelong learners, effective problem solvers and decision makers, able to communicate with a diverse population and to understand how to live successfully in a rapidly changing, high-tech world.

In the words of Sylvia Robinson, *"Some people think you are strong when you hold on. Others think it is when you let go."*

How strong are we?

## REFERENCES

Argyris, C., & Schön, D. (1974). *Theory in practice: Increasing professional effectiveness.* San Francisco, CA: Jossey Bass.

Conley, D. T. (2010). *Redefining college readiness.* Eugene, OR: Education Policy Improvement Center.

Conley, D. T. (2013). Rethinking the notion of "noncognitive." *Education Week.* Retrieved from, http://www.edweek.org/ew/articles/2013/01/23/18conley.h32.html

Friedman, T. (2012). *That used to be us.* New York, NY: Farrar, Straus, & Giroux.

Gallup, Inc. (2013). 21st Century Skills and the Workplace: A 2013 Microsoft Partners in Learning and Pearson Foundation Study. Gallup-Microsoft-Pearson Report. Retrieved from http://www.gallup.com/strategicconsulting/162821/21st-century-skills-workplace.aspx

Lucas, B., Claxton, G., & Spencer, R. (2013). *Expansive education teaching learners for the real world.* Melbourne: Australian Council for Educational Research/Maidenhead: Open University Press.

Mansilla, V. B., & Jackson, A. (2011). *Educating for global competence: Preparing our youth to engage the world.* New York, NY: Council of Chief State School Officers' Ed Steps Initiative & Asia Society Partnership for Global Learning.

Pink, D. (2009). *Drive: The surprising truth about what motivates us.* New York, NY: Penguin.

Resnick, L. (1999). Making America smarter. *Education Week* Century Series, *18*(40), 38–40.

Ritchhart, R. (2002). *Intellectual character: What it is, why it matters, and how to get it.* San Francisco, CA: Jossey Bass.

Roth, M. (2012, September 8). Learning as freedom. *New York Times.* Retrieved from, http://www.nytimes.com/2012/09/06/opinion/john-deweys-vision-of- learning-freedom.html?_r=2&ref=opinion& http://twitter.com/aacu/status/2437192 NOI 21408841728

Seiger-Eherenberg, S. (1991). Educational outcomes for a K–12 curriculum. In Costa, A. (Ed.), *Developing minds: A resource book for teaching thinking.* Alexandria, VA: Association for Supervision and Curriculum Development.

Tough, P. (2012). *How children succeed.* New York, NY: Houghton Mifflin Harcourt.

U. S. Department of Education. Office of Educational Technology. (2013, February 14). *Promoting grit, tenacity, and perseverance: Critical factors of success in the 21st century.* Washington, DC: Center for Technology in Learning, SRI International.

Wagner, T. (2008). *The global achievement gap: Why even our best schools don't teach the new survival skills our children need—And what we can do about it.* New York, NY: Basic Books.

CHAPTER THREE

# What Are Dispositions?

As is often the case, there are many paths to take as long as we are clear about our direction. So it is with dispositions. The term may come by many names: inclination, mindset, tendency, propensity, predilection, proneness, habit, characteristic, penchant, capability, aptness, potential, leaning, proclivity, urge, affinity, affection, and so on. They all are aiming in the same direction. We might hear someone say, "She has a sunny disposition." In this book, we offer a definition for thinking dispositions and provide numerous examples of lists from writers from the fields of philosophy, psychology, education, and science. Each of these lists suggests some different paths leading to the development of dispositional thinking. We specifically call them paths because they represent journeys of exploration that resonate with different cultures, communities, and schools based on the populations they are serving. A path is distinguished from a program in that there is no prescription for which of the dispositions will best match the needs of your students and school community. Rather, we are inviting you to go through the arduous task of learning about many different perspectives/ paths and finally designing a process for deciding which of the stepping-stones best fit your journey.

We provide examples of how teaching dispositional thinking is being embraced in emerging countries around the world. We also share the findings from conversations with hundreds of

18

teachers from various cultures and geographic global regions who describe their dispositional desires for their students.

## DEFINING DISPOSITIONS

According to Wikipedia, a disposition is a habit, a preparation, a state of readiness, or a tendency to act in a specified way. When we use the term "dispositions," we are referring to *thinking dispositions*—tendencies toward particular patterns of intellectual behavior.

Philosopher Robert Ennis, professor emeritus from the University of Illinois, has made significant contributions to our understanding of critical thinking. Ennis (1996) defines a thinking disposition as a tendency to do something given certain conditions. Ennis argues, however, that the disposition must be exercised reflectively. In other words, given the appropriate conditions, dispositions are not automatic.

Stephen Norris (1992), another philosopher of education, defines a thinking disposition as a tendency to think in a certain way under certain circumstances. He suggests that a thinking disposition is not simply a desire or predilection to thinking critically. Rather, individuals must either have formed habits to use certain abilities or overtly think and choose to use the abilities they possess. A person with an *ability* to think critically under certain conditions will do it only if so disposed.

Like Norris, Israeli psychologist Gavriel Salomon regards thinking dispositions as not just a summary label for a cluster in interrelated and relatively stable behaviors (Salomon, 1994). He suggests that dispositions do more than describe behavior; they assume a causal function and have an explanatory status. A disposition is a cluster of preferences, attitudes, and intentions, plus a set of capabilities that allow the preferences to become realized in a particular way.

Skillful thinkers, therefore, have both thinking abilities *and* thinking dispositions. In other words, the critical thinker who seeks balanced reasons in an argument has both the ability and the disposition to do so. Skillful listeners, for example, not only have (1) the ability to listen well, (2) they are also inclined to do so (3) when a situation presents itself (Swartz et al., 2007).

In an effort to explain the basic psychology of thinking dispositions, Perkins, Jay, and Tishman (1993) have put forth what they call a "triadic conception of thinking dispositions." They propose three psychological components that logically must be present to spark dispositional behavior: (1) *sensitivity*— the perception of the appropriateness of a particular behavior, (2) *inclination*—the felt impetus toward a behavior, and (3) *ability*— the basic capacity to follow through with the behavior. For example, someone who is genuinely disposed to seek balanced reasons in an argument is (1) sensitive to occasions to do so (for instance, while reading a newspaper editorial); (2) feels moved, or inclined, to do so; and (3) has the basic ability to follow through with the behavior, for instance, the person actually identifies the pro and con reasons for both sides of an argument.

While we agree and incorporate the three components described previously, we believe there are at least five additional dimensions that define a thinking disposition. (See also, Anderson, Costa, & Kallick, 2008, and Chapter 6 in this book.)

## EXPLORING DISPOSITIONS

We draw on the work of Ron Ritchhart (2002) from Harvard University and his definition of dispositions:

> Acquired patterns of behavior that are under one's control and will as opposed to being automatically activated. Dispositions are overarching sets of behaviors, not just single specific behaviors. They are dynamic and idiosyncratic in their contextualized deployment rather than prescribed actions to be rigidly carried out. More than desire and will, dispositions must be coupled with the requisite ability. Dispositions motivate, activate, and direct our abilities.

Let us unpack Ritchhart's definition by interpreting, sentence by sentence, the meaning of dispositions that he so richly delivers.

1. Acquired patterns of behavior that are under one's control and will as opposed to being automatically activated.

*Our Interpretation*

Dispositions are acquired. We are not necessarily born with them (although we believe that the capacity and potential for their acquisition is innate), rather, they are learned over time. They are repetitive patterns, not single events or skills. They are under our control; we can consciously, intentionally choose to employ them rather than being mindless habits on autopilot.

2. Overarching sets of behaviors, not just single specific behaviors.

*Our Interpretation*

Dispositions are manifested by a complex integration of several skills or behaviors. Skillful listening, for example, is a complex mix of skills requiring attention to what others are saying, paraphrasing, inquiring, holding your own thoughts in abeyance, self-monitoring, taking turns talking, etc.

3. Dynamic and idiosyncratic in their contextualized deployment rather than prescribed actions to be rigidly carried out.

*Our Interpretation*

There are no recipes, prescribed sequences, or scripts for the actions and behaviors of dispositions. Rather they are "maps of the territory" with several pathways leading from where you are to where you hope to be. Furthermore, as we become aware that the territory is changing, so too, must our actions change.

4. More than desire and will, dispositions must be coupled with the requisite ability.

*Our Interpretation*

Not only must we have the desire and yearning to accomplish some task or master some performance, we must also have the skills, capacities, and abilities to do so. (Remember the baseball player who envisioned himself hitting a home run but having no idea of even how to hold, much less swing the bat.)

5. Dispositions motivate, activate, and direct our abilities.

*Our Interpretation*

Directing our abilities implies constant monitoring of our actions and comparing them with our intentions, values, and desires—are we behaving consistently, "walking the talk"? Furthermore, what we are not "up on" we are most likely "down on." Human beings are more likely to act on the beliefs that they embrace. They are more likely to move to action about passions they hold; they are more likely to advocate to others what they are skillful at themselves.

## Dispositions: Some Examples

With all this in mind, what are some examples of dispositions on which to focus and to become the goals of our curriculum, instruction, and assessment? There are many lists and categories. One popular category of thinking dispositions is called "Habits of Mind." According to Lauren Resnick, "The sum of one's intelligence is the sum of one's habits of mind" (2001, p. 4). Theodore Sizer (1992) defines "habits of mind" as the willingness to use one's mind well when no one is looking.

Deborah Meier (2011) (a noted educational reformer, writer, and activist) believes that schools should teach students a specific set of skills in order to be highly effective. The skills, also known as Habits of Mind, include the following:

Significance (Why it is important?)

Perspective (What is the point of view?)

Evidence (How do you know?)

Connection (How does it apply?)

Supposition (What if it were different?)

Costa and Kallick (2008) list 16 Habits of Mind derived from studies of successful, efficient problem solvers from many walks of life (Costa, 2001).

1. *Persisting:* persevering on a task through to completion; remaining focused. *Stick to it!*

2. *Managing impulsivity:* thinking before acting; remaining calm, thoughtful, and deliberative. *Take your time!*

3. *Listening with understanding and empathy:* devoting mental energy to another person's thoughts and ideas; holding in abeyance one's own thoughts to perceive another's point of view and emotions. *Understand others!*

4. *Thinking flexibly:* being able to change perspectives, generate alternatives, and consider options. *Look at it another way!*

5. *Thinking about your thinking (metacognition):* being aware of one's own thoughts, strategies, feelings, and actions and their effects on others. *Know your knowing!*

6. *Striving for accuracy and precision:* having a desire for exactness, fidelity, and craftsmanship. *Check it again!*

7. *Questioning and problem posing:* having a questioning attitude; knowing what data are needed and developing questioning strategies to produce those data. Finding problems to solve. *How do you know?*

8. *Applying past knowledge to novel situations:* accessing prior knowledge; transferring knowledge beyond the situation in which it was learned. *Use what you learn!*

9. *Thinking and communicating with clarity and precision:* striving for accurate communication in both written and oral form; avoiding overgeneralizations, distortions, and deletions. *Be clear!*

10. *Gathering data through all senses:* gathering data through all the sensory pathways—gustatory, olfactory, tactile, kinesthetic, auditory, and visual. *Use your natural pathways!*

11. *Creating, imagining, and innovating:* generating new and novel ideas, fluency, and originality. *Try a different way!*

12. *Responding with wonderment and awe:* finding the world awesome, mysterious and being intrigued with phenomena and beauty. *Have fun figuring it out!*

13. *Taking responsible risks:* being adventuresome; living on the edge of one's competence. *Venture out!*

14. *Finding humor:* finding the whimsical, incongruous, and unexpected. Being able to laugh at oneself. *Laugh a little!*

15. *Thinking interdependently:* being able to work with and learn from others in reciprocal situations. *Work/learn together!*

16. *Remaining open to continuous learning:* having humility and pride when admitting we don't know; resisting complacency. *Learn from experiences!*

Peter and Noreen Facione speak of an overarching disposition to think critically and aim to measure it in their California Critical Thinking Dispositions Inventory (Facione & Facione, 1992). An analysis of their results indicates that this overarching disposition factors into seven subdispositions: (1) open-mindedness, (2) inquisitiveness, (3) systematicity, (4) analyticity, (5) truth seeking, (6) critical thinking self-confidence, and (7) maturity (Facione, Sánchez, Facione, & Gainen, 1995).

Robert Ennis (1996) recognizes 14 separate critical thinking dispositions:

- Be clear about the intended meaning of what is said, written, or otherwise communicated
- Determine and maintain focus on the conclusion or question
- Take the total situation into account
- Seek and offer reasons
- Try to be well informed
- Look for alternatives
- Seek as much precision as the situation requires
- Try to be reflectively aware of one's basic beliefs
- Be open-minded: Seriously consider other points of view and be willing to consider changing your position
- Withhold judgment when the evidence and reasons are sufficient to do so
- Use one's critical thinking abilities
- Be careful
- Take into account the feelings and thoughts of other people

Perkins, Jay, and Tishman (1993) advanced a view of seven key critical thinking dispositions. Building on their triadic conception of disposition, they argue that each of these seven tendencies involves distinct sensitivities, inclinations, and abilities. The seven dispositions are as follows:

1. The disposition to be broad and adventurous
2. The disposition toward wondering, problem finding, and investigating
3. The disposition to build explanations and understandings
4. The disposition to make plans and be strategic
5. The disposition to be intellectually careful
6. The disposition to seek and evaluate reasons
7. The disposition to be metacognitive

In their book *The Learning Powered School,* Claxton, Chambers, Powell, and Lucas (2011) identify 17 thinking dispositions. They are based on 4Rs, each of which is differentiated into four or five more specific learning capacities, or, informally, learning muscles. These are summarized here:

*Resilience*: Being ready, willing, and able to lock on to learning

Absorption: Flow, the pleasure of being rapt in learning

Managing distractions: Recognizing and reducing distractions

Noticing: Really sensing what's out there

Perseverance: Stickability; tolerating the feelings of learning

*Resourcefulness:* Being ready, willing, and able to learn in different ways

Questioning: Getting below the surface; playing with situations

Making links: Seeking coherence, relevance, and meaning

Imagining: Using the mind's eye as a learning theatre

Reasoning: Thinking rigorously and methodically

Capitalizing: Making good use of resources

*Reflectiveness:* Being ready, willing, and able to become more strategic about learning

Planning: Working learning out in advance monitoring

Revising: Monitoring and adapting along the way

Distilling: Drawing out the lessons from experience

Metalearning: Understanding learning and yourself as a learner

*Reciprocity:* Being ready, willing, and able to learn alone and with others

Interdependence: Balancing self-reliance and sociability

Collaboration: The skills of learning with others

Empathy and listening: Getting inside others' minds

Imitation: Picking up others' habits and values

The late Ted Sizer, educational reformer and founder of the Coalition of Essential Schools, also has a list of dispositions that he called habits (Sizer, 1992). He believed that a wise school's goal is to get its students into good intellectual habits. Which habits can be grist for endless debate, but the extent of agreement among Americans on these is very high.

*The habit of perspective.* Organizing an argument, read or heard or seen, into its various parts, and sorting out the major from the minor matter within it. Separating opinion from fact and appreciating the value of each.

*The habit of analysis.* Pondering each of these arguments in a reflective way, using such logical, mathematical, and artistic tools as may be required to render evidence. Knowing the limits as well as the importance of such analysis.

*The habit of imagination.* Being disposed to evolve one's own view of a matter, searching for both new and old patterns that serve well one's own and others' current and future purposes.

*The habit of empathy.* Sensing other reasonable views of a common predicament, respecting all, and honoring the most persuasive among them.

*The habit of communication.* Accepting the duty to explain the necessary in ways that are clear and respectful both to those hearing or seeing and to the ideas being communicated. Being a good listener.

*The habit of commitment.* Recognizing the need to act when action is called for; stepping forward in response. Persisting, patiently, as the situation may require.

*The habit of humility.* Knowing one's rights, one's debts, and one's limitations, and those of others. Knowing what one knows and what one does not know. Being disposed and able to gain the needed knowledge, and having the confidence to do so.

*The habit of joy.* Sensing the wonder and proportion in worthy things and responding to these delights.

Sizer (1992) suggests that habit, obviously, relates to disposition: I have to want to apply these skills. Therefore, I must be convinced of their use and reasonableness. Good schools endlessly labor at this task of persuasion. Good schools self-consciously display these habits in their own functioning. Everything about these schools reinforces the argument that the habits are worthwhile.

These habits reflect value. They neither denote nor connote mere technical expertise, usable skills. They are loaded with judgments, for teachers and parents as well as for students. The lines between habits that are good and bad, slovenly and devoted, personal and collective are blurred. There is no escaping this. A school devoted to the inculcation of certain sorts of intellectual habits—the qualities of mind that engender respect—will tangle endlessly, and revealingly for their students, over matters of judgment. Good schools welcome this. In fact, only from such tangling can those habits we most respect emerge.

Good schools focus on habits, on what sorts of intellectual activities will and should inform their graduates' lives. Not being clear about these habits leads to mindlessness, to institutions that drift along doing what they do simply because they have always done it that way. Such places are full of silly compromises, of practices that boggle commonsense analysis. And they dispirit those who know that the purpose of education is not in keeping students in school but rather in pushing them out into the world as young citizens who are soaked in habits of thoughtfulness and reflectiveness, joy, and commitment. Further, mindless schools may show students a superficial picture of that which is to be most highly valued, whom the school puts forward as its most respected students. Kids with high scores may be ridiculed, human jealousy being what it is. But they will fare much better in a school that knows that the display of knowledge, however accurate or rich, in only a beginning. Students who can use knowledge, who are seemingly in the instinctive habit of using it, are the ones deserving of highest honor (Sizer, 1992).

## DISPOSITIONS ARE A PART OF SETTING STANDARDS

The previous lists of desirable dispositions emanate from noted psychologists, educators, philosophers, and futurists. Additionally, many states and national curriculum documents identify similar lists. For example, page 55 of the Australian Curriculum (2012) contains the following statement regarding dispositions:

> Critical and creative thinking are variously characterized by theorists as dispositions (Tishman, Perkins, & Jay, 1993; Ritchhart, Church, & Morrison, 2011), taxonomies of skills (Bloom, Anderson, Krathwohl, et al., 1956), habits and frames of mind (Costa & Kallick, 2009; de Bono, 1976; 1987; Gardner, 1993), thinking strategies (Marzano, Pickering, & Pollock, 2001), and philosophical inquiry (Lipman, Sharp, & Oscanyan, 1980). Each of these approaches has informed the development of the critical and creative thinking capability.
>
> The capability is concerned with the encouragement of skills and learning dispositions or tendencies toward particular patterns of intellectual behavior. These include being broad, flexible, and adventurous thinkers, making plans and being strategic, demonstrating metacognition, and displaying intellectual perseverance and integrity. Students learn to skillfully and mindfully use thinking dispositions or habits of mind such as risk taking and managing impulsivity (Costa & Kallick, 2009) when confronted with problems to which solutions are not immediately apparent.

For numerous additional examples of dispositions found in curriculum documents from around the world (Finland, Singapore, Australia, New Zealand, South Africa, Wales, etc.), please refer to Lucas, Claxton, and Spencer (2013) and Lucas and Claxton (2009). Dispositions are referred to in the U.S. Common Core Standards in places such as, for example, the mathematical practices.

We have reviewed some of the extensive literature that has helped us define the 16 Habits of Mind that are the basis of our research and the practices we draw from for this book.

## DISPOSITIONS: WHAT TEACHERS WANT FOR THEIR STUDENTS—UNIVERSALLY

In our workshops in which we are introducing the 16 Habits of Mind, we usually start with questions for participants to think about and respond to: "What is it about your students that makes you think they need to learn how to think? What do you see them doing, hear them saying, and what are they feeling? And how would you like them to be?" Regardless of their country, their culture, or their language, we get amazingly consistent responses.

| Teachers Say That Their Students: | And They'd Like Them to: |
|---|---|
| Give up easily without trying | Stick to it, try another way, hang in there, remain focused |
| Blurt out answers, start a task without knowing what to do | Think before they act |
| Lack curiosity | Be curious, investigative |
| Are apathetic ("Who cares?") | Be interested, engaged, fascinated, and intrigued |
| Are disrespectful of others | Be empathic, concerned, and listen |
| Can't apply what they have learned | Draw forth and apply their knowledge |
| Are afraid to try | Be adventuresome and risk taking |
| Believe that they lack creativity | Have confidence with their creative talents |
| Are satisfied with sloppy, mediocre work | Have high standards of excellence and craftsmanship |
| Use vague, imprecise language | Think in complete sentences, clear and precise language; offer a rationale or evidence to support their conclusions |
| Are unaware of their own thought processes | Monitor their own problem-solving strategies |

# FROM NAMING TO ACTION

Each of the lists that has been generated by the many authors reviewed previously has named the dispositions believed to be important for the 21st-century learner. We recommend that educators consider a three-step process for deciding which of those dispositions they will incorporate into their school cultures—identifying and naming the dispositions, giving them meaning by defining them as actions, and establishing indicators for measuring growth.

## Identifying the Dispositions

Ask the questions that we have asked so many people around the world: "What is it about your students that makes you think they need to learn how to think? What do you see them doing, hear them saying, and what are they feeling? And how would you like them to be?"

Once you have generated the list of descriptors for how you would like them to be, analyze the list of dispositions you would like them to consider. You should review the lists and synthesize them into one list for you and your school staff, eliminating duplication. As you analyze, correlate the descriptors generated with the names of dispositions from lists reviewed above. Finally, decide what are the most important dispositions that you would like to focus on for your school.

## Defining Dispositions as Actions

Once you have made a decision, there is a need to move from naming to action. The essential question is, "How do you make the disposition come alive in the minds of students?" Once you've named them, the question is how to give them meaning, build capacities, sensitize students to situations, give them strategies, help them see the value, build commitment to improvement, and move to action that circles back to assessment.

Defining the disposition as actions creates a more vivid picture inside the mind of the learners as to what they will be doing, saying, or feeling if they are performing the disposition. It is more likely that we can agree on actions than on definitions.

Translating the labels of the dispositions into actions and tactics by asking students to envision what they would see people doing or hear them saying if they are, for example, accurate and precise, empathic, or curious. For insights to be useful, they need to be generated from within, not given to individuals as conclusions. This is true for several reasons. First, people will experience the adrenaline-like rush of insight only if they go through the process of making connections themselves.

In addition, this would be true for breaking an old habit as well. When students envision what a disposition looks like and sounds like, it makes possible the elimination of undesirable habits. Change requires observing the pattern that we presently have and then making a conscious decision to break that pattern. We can put our attention to what was missing. We can begin to attend to changing our dispositions and seeing the benefit when we do so (Davidson, 2013).

## Identifying Indicators
## for Measuring Growth

We encourage teachers and curriculum workers to ask students to envision what they would see people doing or hear them saying if they are, for example, persistent, flexible, risk taking, or curious. The poster in Figure 3.1 is from Sarah Evans's third-grade classroom at the Palm Beach Day Academy in Florida. The students "unpack" the behaviors of the disposition, *listening with understanding and empathy.*

## SUMMARY

In this chapter, we have defined what are dispositions, provided many examples, and shown compelling support of dispositional teaching from leaders as well as international curriculum ministries, organizations, and initiatives. We hope that we have not given you cognitive indigestion as you have devoured the many rich ideas in this buffet of possible dispositions. Rather, we suggest that you choose some that make the most sense to you and read on as you learn more about how to operationalize dispositions as a necessary part of your work. Of greatest support is what

**Figure 3.1**  Listening With Understanding and Empathy

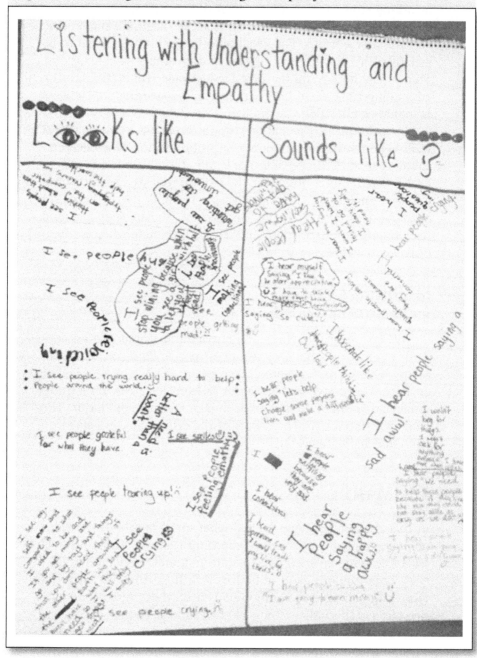

Courtesy, Palm Beach Academy, Palm Beach, Florida

classroom teachers say when we ask them why, if this is the way they would like to see their students develop, they do not include these attributes in their curriculum, instruction, and assessments. They tell us they do not have time. Labeling dispositions with the hope that students will cultivate and develop those attributes when they are called on to be effective communicators, creative and critical thinkers, and collaborate with one another just won't work.

Dispositions must be brought to students' conscious level through defining the behaviors associated with them. If this is what we truly value, we must make the time for including them in curriculum, instruction, and assessment. These are the dispositions of the future and students need to learn them now. As John Cage (1912–1992) said, "I can't understand why people are frightened by new ideas. I'm frightened of old ones."

## REFERENCES

Anderson, J., Costa, A., & Kallick. B. (2008). 5 dimensions of growth. In Costa, A. & Kallick, B. (Eds.), *Learning and leading with Habits of Mind: Sixteen characteristics of success.* Alexandria, VA: ASCD.

Australian Curriculum and Reporting Authority. (2012). *The Australian Curriculum.* Canberra, Australia.

Costa, A. (2001) Habits of Mind. In Costa, A. (Ed). *Developing minds: A Resource book for teaching thinking.* Alexandria, VA: ASCD.

Costa, A., & Kallick, B. (2008). *Learning and leading with Habits of Mind: Sixteen characteristics of success.* Alexandria, VA: ASCD.

Claxton, G., Chambers, M., Powell, G., & Lucas, B. (2011). *The learning powered school: Pioneering 21st century education.* Bristol, England: TLO Limited.

Davidson, C. (2013). *Now you see it: How the brain science of attention will transform the way we live, work, and learn.* New York, NY: Viking Press.

Ennis, R. H. (1996). Critical thinking dispositions: Their nature and accessibility. *Informal Logic, 18*(2 & 3), 165–182.

Facione, P. A., & Facione N. C. (1992). *The California critical thinking dispositions inventory.* Millbrae, CA: California Academic Press.

Facione, P. A., Sánchez, C. A., Facione, N. C., & Gainen, J. (1995). The disposition toward critical thinking. *Journal of General Education, 44*(1), 1–25.

Lucas, B., & Claxton, G. (2009). *Wider skills for learning: What are they, how can they be cultivated, how could they be measured and why are they important for innovation:* The Centre for Real-World Learning,

University of Winchester, UK. Retrieved from, www.winchester.ac
.uk/realworldlearning

Lucas, B., Claxton, G., and Spencer, E. (2013). *Expansive education: Teaching learners for the real world.* Bristol, England: TLO Limited.

Meier, D. (2011). 5 habits of mind. Retrieved from, http://21century
schools.wordpress.com/2011/06/28/5-habits-of-mind-debroah-
meier/

Norris, S. P. (Ed.). (1992). *The generalizability of critical thinking: Multiple perspectives on an educational ideal.* New York, NY: Teachers College Press.

Perkins, D. N., Jay, E., & Tishman, S. (1993). Beyond abilities: A disposi-tional theory of thinking. *Merrill-Palmer Quarterly: Journal of Developmental Psychology, 39*(1), 1–21. Retrieved from, http://psyc
net.apa.org/psycinfo/1993–20281–001

Resnick, L. (2001). Making America smarter: The real goal of school reform. In Costa, A. (Ed.), *Developing minds: A resource book for teach-ing thinking.* Alexandria, VA: ASCD.

Ritchhart, R. (2002). *Intellectual character: What it is, why it matters, and how to get it.* San Francisco, CA: Jossey Bass.

Salomon, G. (1994). *Interaction of media, cognition and Learning: An explo-ration of how symbolic forms cultivate mental skills and affect knowledge acquisition.* New York, NY: Routledge.

Sizer, T. (1992). *Horace's school: Redesigning the American high school.* New York, NY: Houghton Mifflin.

Swartz, R., Costa, A., Beyer, B., Reagan, R., & Kallick, B. (2007). *Thinking based learning: Promoting quality student achievement in the 21st cen-tury.* New York, NY: Teachers College Press.

CHAPTER FOUR

# Deciding on Dispositions

In Chapter 3, we overwhelmed and maybe exhausted your brain with numerous lists of thinking dispositions, Habits of Mind, critical thinking skills, clusters of preferences, attitudes, and intentions. While all the dispositions listed are important, many overlap, and they certainly cannot all be taught. Choices must be made. Different dispositions are needed as students mature, as different content is taught, and as different school values are considered. Major decisions, therefore, that teachers and school staffs must make are the following:

- Which of these dispositions should be adopted, emphasized, and attention focused on?
- When and in what sequences should they be taught?
- Under what conditions should students encounter them?
- How is it best to keep the whole system organized so that there is integration, sequencing, and building on previous experience?

This chapter explores how we decide.

You may wish to choose one of the sets of dispositions, such as the list by Guy Claxton in *Building Learning Power* or by Ted Sizer's *Habits* or Ennis's *Critical Thinking Dispositions* or Costa and Kallick's *Habits of Mind*. As you discovered, these lists are similar. What is important in deciding which list to adopt is that a staff builds commitment to them, that they are relevant and make sense to the teachers, and that the staff is willing to implement them consistently and collaboratively throughout the grade levels and subject areas. What gives the dispositions their power is that the staff and community share them as the desired characteristics of the graduates of the school system. A commitment must also be made to decide on and use a common vocabulary so students will encounter those dispositions repeatedly throughout their school day, in all their classes, in all subject areas, and in each succeeding year in school. Staff members must be willing to include dispositions as part of their lesson design and to assess students' growth in the dispositions over time. Furthermore, such decisions imply that individual members of the staff are willing to model those dispositions not only in the presence of their students but also as norms of the school. Staff members must commit to monitor and grow their dispositions right along with their students.

Obviously all the dispositions on the list cannot be emphasized at the same time. Once a list has been compiled and a commitment made by the staff to implement that list, some additional decisions will need to be made about which dispositions will be focused on and when. Observing your students as they confront challenging tasks and work though projects can yield valuable diagnostic data to help with the following decisions. We suggest five basic sources for these decisions: (1) In which dispositional gifts do your students excel and how might you build on these to make them even more conscious and skillful? (2) Which dispositions do your students need along their journey from childhood to maturity? (3) Which dispositions does your school or institution value, celebrate, and advocate? (4) Which dispositions will enable and facilitate the learning of the content being taught? (5) Which dispositions do the scholars in that discipline practice?

## In which dispositional gifts do your students excel?

While students may not have been taught directly nor do they know the names of the dispositions, many children bring with them dispositional gifts. They are naturally curious, adventuresome, and humorous, for example. The challenge is to recognize and exalt these attributes as well as to build on them to make them even more conscious and skillful?

## Which dispositions do your students need?

The major source of important dispositions for your students is to observe them as they work in groups, as they confront rigorous problems, as they respond to conflicts, and as they make decisions. In Chapter 2 challenging questions were posed. To decide on which dispositions your students need, we invite you to respond again: "What is it about your students that makes you think they need to learn how to think?" "What do you see them doing, hear them saying, and feeling?" "And how would you like them to be?"

| We Observe Our Students | Disposition They Might Need |
|---|---|
| Giving up easily without trying | Perseverance |
| Blurting out answers, start a task without knowing what to do | Managing their impulsivity |
| Lacking curiosity | Questioning |
| Responding with apathy, ("Who cares") ("It's boring") | Finding wonderment and awe |
| Being disrespectful of others | Listening with understanding and empathy |
| Unable to apply what they have learned | Drawing on prior knowledge and applying it to new situations |
| Afraid to try | Being adventuresome, risk taking |
| Believing that they lack creativity | Creating imagining and innovating |
| Being satisfied with sloppy, mediocre work | Striving for craftsmanship |
| Using vague, imprecise language, "Ya' know," "er," "stuff," "things" | Using clear and precise language |
| Unaware of their own thought processes | Metacognition: Thinking about their thinking |

While this list is not complete, the intent here is to start with your students. Which dispositions do they need?

With the dispositions in mind as a filter, you will soon focus on individual students as well as groups:

Juan Carlos is a loner. During recess he usually sits on the bench by himself. He needs to be accepted and work and play with others—*to think interdependently.*

*"I don't get it,"* says Alexander. He reads the directions again and says, "I don't get it." My frustration, however, is that he doesn't seem to care whether he gets it or not. He thinks that because he "doesn't get it," he doesn't need to "get it." It's easier for him to give up when he's confronted with an obstacle. He won't even try. He needs to learn how to *persist!*

And Tamika is so solemn. She never smiles. When the other kids are laughing, she usually lowers her eyes. She needs to *find humor and joy.*

Then there is Jasper. Have you seen his desk? Papers and books are jammed in, he can't find anything, and he cares little whether his papers are neat or even if he has completed the assignment. He needs a strong dose of *craftsmanship.*

## Which dispositions do your school, institution, and community value?

In discussions among members of school staffs, agreements are made that particular groups or age levels of students need certain dispositions. Thus, entire grade-level groups or the total staff agree that they will focus on one or two dispositions needing their greatest attention for a period of time (month, semester, or term). For example, primary teachers in one school realized their kindergartners and first graders, being highly ego-centered at this age, needed to manage their impulsivity, learn to listen to and empathize with others, and (because these students came from impoverished home backgrounds where there were language deficits), use clear and precise language.

It was also interesting that these teachers were aware of their primary children's dispositional strengths: The children were naturally curious, they used all their senses, they were wondrous and inquisitive, and they were exceedingly adventuresome. The teachers' chief concern was how to keep these dispositions "alive" as the students advanced to higher grade levels.

The primary grade teachers from yet another school observed that some students from affluent homes seemed to lack the inclination for problem finding and problem solving. From parent conferences, staff members offered examples of overprotective nannies and "helicopter moms" who "hovered" over their children, protecting them from experiencing failure or being in need. Their children grew up expecting others to do everything from tying their shoes and cutting their pancakes to deciding on the clothes to wear. Thus, when confronted with problematic situations, the children depended on others to solve their problems rather than taking the initiative to solve their own problems. The staff decided to focus on the dispositions of *problem finding, problem solving,* and *persisting* as the paramount needs of these students.

The upper-grade teachers agreed that their fourth- and fifth-grade students needed to be more conscious of their own thinking. When asked, for example, to explain how they arrived at an answer, the students typically responded, "I don't know. I just did it." The grade-level group decided to focus on *metacognition* to cause them to think about, become more conscious of, and reflect on their thinking before, during, and after solving a problem or working on a complex, struggle-rich task.

A middle school staff was concerned about some of their students' apathy toward learning, and many of the staff reported that students often responded to their learning with such comments as, "Who cares" or "When will I ever need this," or "This is boring." This behavior prompted the middle school staff to adopt the disposition *finding wonderment and awe* as the focus for the semester. They generated vocabulary lists to describe their wonderment (e.g., fascinated. mesmerized, attracted, dazzled, astonished, and enthralled). They talked about what goes on in their heads when and how they become fascinated (the "wow" factor). They found and brought to class examples of beauty on the Internet, in books, and in the environment. They took nature walks and kept "noticing notebooks" of objects and events that caught their eye or caused them to ponder, to question, and to look again. (Appreciation to Scott Wright, North Syracuse School District, New York, for these ideas.)

A high school staff found that their preadolescents were a bit too risk taking. From their readings and studies of neuroscience and the teenage brain, the teachers knew that the frontal cortex—the seat of judgment, self-control, and sensible planning—matures very gradually into early adulthood. It is out of sync with the early development of the emotional brain, and as a result, there is a gap between early sensation seeking and later self-discipline. Teenagers are attracted to novel and risky activities, especially with peers, at a time when they lack judgment and the ability to weigh future consequences. The staff decided to focus on *managing/controlling impulses* and to teach the difference between risk taking and "*responsible* risk taking."

In another school in a very affluent, high-socioeconomic community, the staff agreed that, while the students scored well on achievement tests, all students graduated, and most went on to complete college, they lacked the disposition of "thinking outside the box." When they brought this condition to the students' attention, these high schoolers admitted that they were afraid of being wrong. They felt more comfortable in providing "correct" answers or responses that they thought would receive commendation from the teachers. "Why don't you just tell us the answer?" many students would say.

The staff decided that the disposition of thinking creatively would be paramount for these students. They started by showing the movie *Apollo 13* (See the *Teachers Companion*, 2013) and invited students to observe and comment on the creative problem solving of the crew. They conducted lessons in which students learned to monitor their creative thought processes when engaging in such strategies of creative thinking as SCAMPER, synectics, brainstorming, word games, metaphorical thinking, and the like (Ferlazzo, 2013). The staff also decided to help students become aware of their creative thinking outside of school by monitoring their thinking over time, since creative thought often is most acute early in the morning, while asleep, or in moments of solitude—encouraging our subconscious mind to work for us. (For even greater detail on Habits of Mind and creativity, see Donald J. Treffinger's article in *Educational Leadership*, "Preparing Creative and Critical Thinkers," Summer 2008, Volume 65, Thinking Skills NOW [online only].)

The teachers also asked themselves which dispositions they needed to employ to create school and classroom conditions that would foster a safe environment so students would more likely think creatively and express their divergent ideas. The teachers decided that they needed three dispositions themselves: (1) listening with empathy and without judgments, (2) flexibility to accept and support students' divergent learning styles and forms of expression, and of course, (3) the teachers themselves would need to model creating or imagining innovating themselves and reinforce it when observed in others.

The parents of another school were concerned about bullying, both cyberbullying and face-to-face bullying. Obviously, students lacked respect, empathy, and flexibility in knowing how to accept other's differences. The staff decided to focus on three areas that bullies lacked: learning abilities, self-management, and interpersonal love. Specifically they focused on *the learning abilities* of *persisting, striving for accuracy,* and *thinking and communicating with clarity and precision.* The *self-management* dispositions included *metacognition, managing impulsivity,* and *responding with wonderment and awe.*

The staff decided that these students who were bullies lacked abilities of *giving and receiving love.* They focused, therefore, on *listening with understanding and empathy, flexibility,* and *thinking interdependently.* (Appreciation for these ideas is expressed to Lewis Alberto Mendoza, Counselor, Chester E. Jordan Elementary School, Socorro School District El Paso, Texas.)

Another high school staff adopted the program *Philosophy for Children.* This strategy requires students to listen attentively to each other with understanding and empathy, to respect each others' ideas, to paraphrase to show their understanding, to take turns talking, and to respond nonjudgmentally to other's ideas even though their ideas may differ from theirs. They read and discussed Charles Derber's (1979) book, *The Pursuit of Attention: Power and Ego in Everyday Life,* and explored the meaning of his term "conversational narcissism" and how effective listeners keep the focus on the listener rather than shifting the response to a personal (autobiographical) reference.

## Which dispositions will enable and facilitate the learning of the content?

As you design your lessons and units and decide on which dispositions you wish students to practice, it is also helpful to think about which dispositions will facilitate the activity of learning. For example, in preparation for a laboratory science activity, the science teacher might alert students to the fact that they will be working in groups in their lab stations. The teacher might say,

"Since you'll be working in groups, let's think about thinking interdependently. What might that look like or sound like as you work through your experiment?"

Or in preparation for a field trip to the nature area, a primary teacher might ask the students to think about what they will be doing if they are gathering data through all senses and how they might be aware of their wonderment, intrigue, and awe. Or for a math lesson, the teacher might alert students that this new problem will challenge them to apply their past knowledge to this new situation. They will need to persist and to develop alternative metacognitive approaches to solving the problem

## Which dispositions are exemplary of the scholars in that discipline?

The Habits of Mind dispositions synthesized by Costa (2001) were derived from studies of effective problem solvers from many disciplines, professions, and walks of life: entrepreneurs, artists, teachers, lawyers, plumbers, and auto mechanics. Dispositions, therefore, can be found across all content areas. (See Costa & Kallick, 2008.) Many curricula, including Common Core State Standards, the International Baccalaureate, and Advanced Placement, invite students to "think like a scientist." Thinking like a scientist, a historian, a mathematician, an artist, a writer, an anthropologist, or a chef, for that matter (see "Cooking Habits" by Nicholas D'Aglas, 2008), means confronting the challenges of that discipline and then doing what the scholar does: asking questions that can be answered based on evidence, expressing questions in a way that allows someone to check your work, gathering data through all senses, listening to others, striving for accuracy, being continuous learners, and finding wonderment and awe in the chosen profession or field of work.

This essential question creates a mindshift for students. They are no longer just memorizing the parts of the plant. They are experiencing the dispositions necessary to think like a scientist: taking responsible risks, gathering data using all of the senses, communicating with clarity and precision, observing, experimenting, collecting data, and thinking about the data that they collect.

Of course, if you want students to think like scientists, they need some scientific problems to think about. In the past, scholars

**Figure 4.1**   Think Like a Scientist

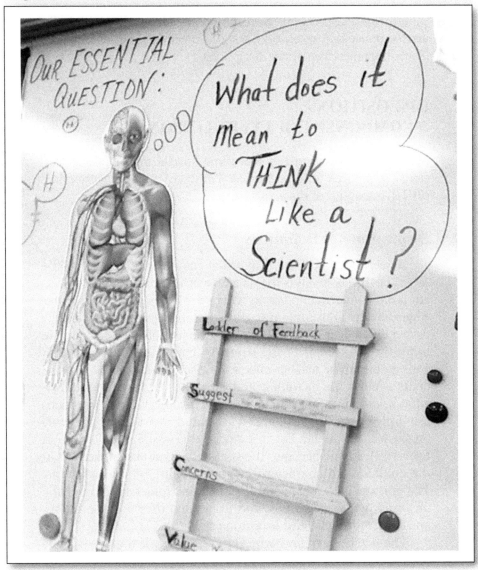

Appreciation for this poster to Laura Jane Louck, Palm Beach Academy, Palm Beach, Florida.

were skillful in answering questions and solving problems in their particular discipline, in part, because they had information. Today, they must be good at thinking across disciplines, problem finding, asking questions, uncovering possibilities, surfacing latent issues, and anticipating unexpected problems (Pink, 2012, p. 132). To think like a historian, then, requires that students raise some historical problems to think about. Likewise, to think like artists, musicians, or economists, they need to generate and confront challenges from those disciplines.

## DISPOSITIONS: A COMPONENT OF EVERY LESSON

Dispositional teaching requires some special instructional decisions, sequences, and strategies. We draw on Nancy Skerritt's (2010) metaphor of the actors in a play.

### Dispositions as Definitive

At certain times, the disposition may be thought of as the "star" of the show—it is the objective of the lesson, and we present a direct instruction lesson where the disposition takes center stage. Subject area content in these lessons becomes a vehicle for developing a deep understanding of the identified disposition. To bring the disposition to the students' conscious awareness and consideration, the teacher makes the disposition explicit. The students explore the definition and attributes of the disposition— what it looks like and sounds like and its application. They focus primarily on the disposition, just as an audience focuses primarily on the leads in a play. For this day, in this lesson, the disposition takes the lead and becomes the star, with all attention directed at the qualities and characteristics that the disposition represents. The purpose is to build consciousness and understanding of the meaning of the disposition and to develop the capacities, tools, and tactics to employ the disposition skillfully.

The teacher explains why the disposition is important. The purpose of the *explanation* is to ensure that students are directly provided with information about the core concepts and methods of the thinking disposition. Students should be provided with explanations about such concepts as evidence, hypothesis, justification, and theory. And they should also be provided with explanations about methods for seeking evidence and constructing hypotheses.

## Dispositions as Supportive

At other times, dispositions may be like the members of the cast—they serve in a supportive role. The disposition is woven throughout the lesson, reinforcing the content as a tool to foster understanding. While the students are working to understand the content, the teacher my alert them to the need for employing the disposition (listening with empathy, for example) and may recognize the students as they display evidence of using the disposition. The purpose is to reinforce, internalize, and call attention to the benefits and appropriate circumstances in which to employ the disposition.

## Dispositions as Reflective

At still other times, the dispositions may be in the background—as members of the ensemble. Great productions require quality ensembles to build depth and provide background. Without the support of minor characters, a play would fall flat. While we may not see a certain character with frequency in a show, we are very much aware of the character's contribution in the scenes where that individual plays a role. Likewise, the dispositions bring value added to any lesson when the teacher reinforces attitudes, illustrates characteristics in the content, and seeks applications to situations beyond this lesson. The purpose is to metacognitively reflect on the use of the disposition, to recall the mental processes of using ("interiorize") the disposition, to illuminate the value of employing the disposition, and to make application or bridge to other future situations in which the disposition may appropriately be used.

# BECOMING ALERT TO DISPOSITIONS AROUND US

Not only do we want students to become aware of, practice, and apply the dispositions that we think they need, we also encourage students and teachers to remain alert to finding other positive, helpful dispositions throughout the school and home environment—in the newspaper, on television, in the community, and the like.

In her chapter, "Using Habits of Mind to Look 'Inside the Text,'" Kathleen Reilly (2008) invites her high school students to analyze *The Great Gatsby* for the dispositions of the characters.

Judy Roach helped her students find and appreciate dispositions by making connections to the mushers in the grueling Iditarod race in Alaska (See Costa & Kallick, 2008, pp. 77–78).

Many teachers invite their students to find the dispositions of famous people—our heroes and heroines—such as Madame Curie, Leonardo da Vinci, Abraham Lincoln, Thomas Edison, Steve Jobs, Rosa Parks, Martin Luther King, and the like.

Many children's books exemplify the dispositions. *The Little Engine That Could,* for example, illuminates persistence. *The Diary of Anne Frank* is an object lesson in the management of impulsivity and persisting. (For additional examples, go to http://www .instituteforhabitsofmind.com/ Bibliography of Children's Books.)

Films and YouTube presentations are also wonderful sources to illustrate dispositions. Scenes from such films as *Apollo 13,* for example, are a vivid, real adventure of creative problem solving. *Finding Nemo* is an example of persistence. Tom Hanks's compelling scene in *Cast Away* in which he builds a fire is a prime example of persistence.

Quotations provide an impetus for uncovering the meanings of the dispositions. Albert Einstein, for example, said, "The formulation of a problem is often more essential than its solution, which may be merely a matter of mathematical or experimental skill. To raise new questions, new possibilities, to regard old problems from a new angle, requires creative imagination and marks real advances."

Invite students to "unpack" such quotes to seek out examples of dispositions.

For additional ideas, see *Habits of Mind Teacher's Companion* and the quotations resource at www.instituteforhabitsofmind.com.

## NOT JUST KID STUFF

*If there is anything that we wish to change in the child, we should first examine it and see whether it is not something that could better be changed in ourselves.*

—Carl Jung

What gives a curriculum dignity is that it is as good for adults as it is for students. It not just kid stuff. Furthermore, the dispositions are as applicable to developing adult capacities for effective problem solvers and continuous learners as they are to students. All members of the learning organization continue to become more thoughtful. The outcomes for students and the work culture of the school become congruent and synonymous.

No one ever "achieves mastery" of dispositions—they are a work in progress. All of us can continue to perfect our performance, to develop our capacities, to be more alert to opportunities for their use, and to more deliberately employ the dispositions throughout our lifetime. All of us can become continual learners.

Dottin (2010) suggests that excellence in teaching is dispositional. He states, "Intelligent performance is not just an exercise of ability. It is more dispositional in nature in that we must activate abilities and set them in motion. Dispositions concern not only what we can do (our abilities) but what we are actually likely to do" (p. 12). In other words, dispositions must be developed, nurtured, supported, and practiced on a regular basis. Positive dispositions embrace a growth mindset. Schools whose culture teaches, supports, and encourages the use of positive dispositions are more likely to see significant improvement among their teachers than those that do not.

Among the most significant questions that should be asked by those describing teacher quality are the following:

- What is the likelihood they will persevere through disappointment and challenge in their teaching, spending additional time, consulting others, reviewing, and revising their decisions when hoped-for results have not occurred?
- What is the likelihood that in the process of teaching and concentrating on the responses of an individual student they use an eagle view of the classroom to monitor the full class?
- What is the likelihood that a teacher will work diligently to perfect the craft of teaching by adapting to and embracing the changing demands?
- What is the likelihood that faced with a stubborn problem they look at it from various perspectives and can see the perspective of a disappointed parent in a conference?

- What is the likelihood that they will take disappointments in stride and ask themselves how they can cope with and learn from these rather than blaming others?
- What is the likelihood that they will insist on quality performance from themselves and their students and accept nothing less?
- What is the likelihood that they will regard teaching as a collaborative pursuit, engaging with others in applying systemic solutions to persistent problems? (Costa, Garmston, & Zimmerman, 2014)

These are the dispositions of quality teaching. As John Dewey (1933, p. 30) stated, "Knowledge of methods alone will not suffice; there must be the desire, the will to employ them. This desire is an affair of personal disposition."

Might we, as adults, claim to be perfect listeners or to manage our impulsivity even when emotionally flooded or to persist in all endeavors? We can all get better at these dispositions. We can learn right along with the students. We can embark with them on the journey of continuous growth. Furthermore, it behooves parents and teachers to let their children know what dispositions they are working on and to seek their youngster's help by giving feedback and by recognizing instances in which the adult did (or did not) demonstrate the disposition.

## SUMMARY

In this chapter, we explored several decisions that teachers, staffs, and curriculum designers make as they plan for dispositional teaching and learning.

Opportunities to encounter, become more aware of, learn to value, and practice the dispositions are omnipresent throughout the school day, in the classroom and school, in the community, and in society. One has but to pick up the newspaper or watch TV and find examples of local, state, national, and international leaders who may demonstrate (or need to demonstrate) the application of these thinking dispositions.

# REFERENCES

Costa, A. (2001). Habits of Mind. In Costa, A. (Ed.), *Developing minds: A resource book for teaching thinking.* Alexandria, VA: ASCD.

Costa, A., Garmston, R., & Zimmerman, D. (2014). *Cognitive capital: Investing in teacher quality.* New York, NY: Teachers College Press.

Costa, A., & Kallick. B. (Eds.). (2008). *Habits of Mind across the curriculum.* Alexandria, VA: ASCD.

D'Aglas, N. (2008). Cooking habits. In Costa, A., & Kallick, B. (Eds.), *Habits of Mind across the curriculum.* Alexandria, VA: ASCD.

Derber, C. (1979). *The pursuit of attention: Power and ego in everyday life.* New York, NY: Oxford University Press.

Dewey, J. (1933). *How we think: A restatement of the relation of reflective thinking to the educative process.* Boston: D. C. Heath.

Dottin, E. (2010). *Dispositions as habits of Mind: Making professional conduct more intelligent.* Landham, MD: University Press of America.

Ferlazzo, L. (2013). Response: Ways to develop creative thinking in the common core. Retrieved from http://blogs.edweek.org/teachers/classroom_qa_with_larry_ferlazzo/2013/05/response_ways_to_develop_creative_thinking_in_the_common_core.html

Pink, D. (2012). *To sell is human: The surprising truth about moving others.* New York, NY: Riverhead Books.

Reilly, K. C. (2008). Using Habits of Mind to look "inside the text." In Costa, A., & Kallick, B. (Eds.), *Habits of Mind across the curriculum.* Alexandria, VA: ASCD.

Skerritt, N. (2010). Casting call: Enter the Habits of Mind. *Teachers Matter Spectrum Education, 11.*

# Dispositions: Hardwired or Learned?

*Over millions of years of evolution, the brain has grown from the bottom up, with its higher centers developing as elaborations of lower, more ancient parts.*

—Daniel Goleman, *Emotional Intelligence*

The human brain's most amazing feature is its ability to sculpt itself based on its environment. For millions of years the human brain has gradually adapted itself in response to the demands and requirements for survival, its primary purpose. Our earliest ancestors met social, physical, and environmental challenges that still influence human behavior to this day: alertness to subtle threatening cues, nonverbal communications, detection of deception, immediate response to danger signals in the environment, and fulfilling human needs for food, shelter, and water all contribute to the survival of the species. These human capacities are in operation today as we interact with others, with our

We acknowledge and appreciate the work of Pat Wolfe, EdD, brain research translator, author, and educational consultant in Napa, California, for her contributions to this chapter.

modern-day problems, and in response to the current tensions produced by society's dilemmas. Our brain continues in its survival mode—we just face a different set of circumstances in which to survive than did our ancestors.

Educators have become intrigued by the research in the neurosciences and are searching for implications and applications of this research for teaching and learning. We strive to make teaching more brain compatible and believe that as additional research yields insights into how the brain learns, educators will be able to make their instruction more effective. Some dispositions are essential for optimal human development, as they are "hardwired" in our brains and bodies. Simultaneously, we are engaging in an ongoing debate about what learning is of most worth and what students need to know and be able to do today that will be essential and enduring throughout their lifetimes. The purpose of this chapter is to explore the relationships between the dispositions and the research about the human brain and learning.

## DISPOSITIONS: INNATE, LEARNED, OR BOTH?

Frequently, we hear people say, "He just doesn't have any empathy for the situation." Or, "She cannot help being so inflexible. That is just her personality." There has been a great debate about whether dispositions are inherited, can be taught, or perhaps are a combination of the two. We pose an intriguing question: Are dispositions innate—in the genes and chromosomes, or are they a set of strategies, skills, and tactics that can be taught and learned (U.S. Department of Education, Office of Educational Technology, 2013)? Or both? We believe that some dispositions are human capacities that are  hardwired in our brains and bodies. *Capacities* implies that there is the potential for being fulfilled and expanded or for becoming fixed or limited if they are not exercised, practiced, or if environmental conditions stunt their development. Stress, loneliness, and poor health impair the prefrontal functions.

Babies learn fast. By the time infants are three months old, their unfinished brains are laced with a trillion connections, and these connections triple in a year (Mohan, 2013). For example, babies are born with the natural capacity to learn any language. Neuronal connections in their brains are formed through

**Figure 5.1**   Babies are naturally curious, observant, and wondrous. (Alex Wilsey at three months)

hearing, mimicking, and experimenting with sounds. Through neural pruning, they strengthen their use of the language they hear and give up the sounds and patterns they do not hear.

Likewise, all humans, for example, have a natural capacity for creativity. In their early years, however, if children are criticized for thinking differently, if their environments are barren, their natural capacities may be underdeveloped. Humans are born with the capacity of curiosity—to question and to explore. Living in a nonresponsive, barren environment and being admonished for asking questions will soon thwart this tendency. Likewise, when children develop in rich, responsive environments where challenging tasks requiring persistence are given, where children hear complex language, where children have to solve their own problems, then these capacities are developed more fully and are more likely to continue developing over time.

## INNATE DISPOSITIONS OBVIOUS IN THE YOUNG CHILD

*The pursuit of truth and beauty is a sphere of activity in which we are permitted to remain children all our lives.*

—Albert Einstein

Anyone who works with, lives with, or has had children of their own is keenly aware of toddlers' natural-born tendencies and inclinations:

Curiosity and questioning

Constructing self-meaning

Being attracted to and intrigued by phenomena and mystery

Naiveté—remaining open to learning

Self-initiating—internal motivation

Transparency of self—congruence between intentions and actions

Sensory learning—intake through all senses

Openness to feedback—innate desire to improve and achieve

Playfulness—finding humor and joy

Interdependence—turning for guidance, advice, and modeling

Innocence—lacking prejudices, biases, and corruption

As *Homo sapiens* evolved over the years, the presence of these capacities was essential to survival. The brain, being plastic, modified itself to incorporate them into neurons. These dispositions are innate. They are still with us even though the societal and environmental conditions have changed. The real challenge for us as parents and teachers is how to keep our children's natural,

**Figure 5.2**   Wonderment and Awe (Annabelle Wilsey, courtesy her
Mom, Sarah Wilsey)

in-born dispositions alive and well. Once lost, they are hard to
retrieve. Strategies for remedial zest are elusive.

## NINE DISPOSITIONS
## AND THE NEUROSCIENCES

Nine dispositions are presented here because there is neuroscientific research to support them. For other dispositions, while they
may be critical for success in school, work, and life, there is little
neuroscientific research to justify the connection at this time. The
purpose is to demonstrate that these dispositions were not only

crucial for human survival over the centuries and they are also crucial for students' success in school, in later life and careers, and in their survival throughout the 21st and, for some, into the 22nd centuries.

## Metacognition

> *I've reached the moment where the movement of my thought interests me more than the thought itself.*

—Pablo Picasso

Occurring in the neocortex, metacognition is our ability to know what we know and what we don't know. It is the ability of the mind to monitor and redirect the activities of the brain, to plan a strategy for producing what information is needed, to be conscious of our own steps and strategies during the act of problem solving, and to reflect on and evaluate the productiveness of our own thinking (Dunlosky & Metcalf, 2009; Hacker, Dunlosky, & Graesser, 2009).

The major components of metacognition are developing a plan of action, maintaining that plan in mind over a period of time, then reflecting back on and evaluating the plan upon its completion. Planning a strategy before embarking on a course of action assists us in keeping track of the steps in the sequence of planned behavior at the conscious awareness level for the duration of the activity. It facilitates making temporal and comparative judgments, assessing the readiness for more or different activities, and monitoring our interpretations, perceptions, decisions, and behaviors. An example of this would be how teachers develop a teaching strategy for a lesson, keeping that strategy in mind throughout the instruction, then reflecting back on the strategy to evaluate its effectiveness in producing the desired student outcomes.

Intelligent people plan for, reflect on, and evaluate the quality of their own thinking skills and strategies. They are spectators of their own thinking. Metacognition means becoming increasingly aware of one's mental processes and strategies and the effects they produce in others and on the environment; forming internal questions as one searches for information and meaning, developing mental maps or plans of action, mentally rehearsing prior to performance, monitoring those plans as they are employed—being conscious of the need for midcourse correction if the plan is not meeting expectations, reflecting on the plan upon completion of the implementation for the purpose of self-evaluation, and editing mental pictures for improved performance.

## Metacognition and the Brain

Housed in the prefrontal cortex in front of the brain is where such capacities as use of reason, making sense of ideas and behaviors, planning and futuristic thinking, critical and creative thinking, reflection, evaluation, and thinking about our own thinking occur. These are the brain's executive functions.

One of the most amazing characteristics of the brain is that it is the only organ in the body that sculpts itself based on its experiences. This characteristic is called neuroplasticity. For example, while a baby is born with the capacity to speak any of over six thousand languages, the language it hears repeatedly will strengthen certain connections between brain cells, while the connections for the sounds that are not heard or reinforced will eventually fade away. While neuroplasticity has been considered to be most active when a child is young, new research has shown that the brains of older children, as well as those of adults, retain the capacity for rewiring.

Studies show that willful, intentional, mindful effort can alter brain function. Think about it and you will probably be able to think of a time when you changed one of your own habits. If you are like most, this required a great deal of effort and practice using the new set of behaviors before they became automatic. Changing your "clutch behavior" when you move from driving a car with a manual transmission to one with an automatic transmission is an example. The truly amazing thing is that this change in behaviors produced an actual change in the neural connections that control the muscles involved in shifting gears. It probably took quite a while before the new shifting behavior became as automatic as the previous one.

The same is true when we decide to develop or change a disposition. It takes instruction and practice to learn to control impulsivity, to think interdependently, or to listen with understanding and empathy. When an old behavior—such as reacting impulsively—has become an automatic habit, it's not easy to change. The old habit has been reinforced many times and is "hardwired," so to speak. It resists being changed. To replace this behavior with a new one, you literally have to change the wiring of the brain, and this takes time and effort.

## Persisting

*Most of the important things in the world have been accomplished by people who have kept on trying when there seemed to be no hope at all.*

—Dale Carnegie

In a most fundamental way, persistence has been essential to human beings since the dawn of our species. Early man endured perilous climates, uncertain food sources, tribal rivalries, and hungry predators. If they were not persistent in their quest for nourishment and shelter, they died. Anthropologists now believe that persistence played an even more vital role in human development. Without it, we may never have evolved into humans in the first place nor would we have migrated to all parts of the globe.

According to Daniel Lieberman, a professor of human evolutionary biology at Harvard University, humans are one of the few mammals capable of running long distances (marathons) and the only ones who attempt such feats in the heat of the day. Endurance running became a favorite evolutionary trait two million years ago when early man engaged in "persistence hunting."

This technique was used before the invention of tools like bows and arrows or stone-tipped spears and relied on the fact that most animals were only capable of short bursts of speed. Early hunters would jog after large animals for hours until their prey, overheated, collapsed and could be killed with the hunters having little risk of getting injured. Our ancestors were hunting big, prime-age animals with no projectile technology. They would have had to get very close to those animals to kill them, which would have been really dangerous without persistence hunting.

### Persistence and the Brain

Persistence hunters, therefore, provided nearly all the meat for early humans, and of course it was this regular supply of protein-rich meat that allowed our bodies and brains to grow and evolve to the point that we could create tools and develop language—those traits that make us human. Thus, this early persistence laid the groundwork for our most advanced intellectual pursuits. A persistence hunt requires one to make hypotheses, to have a theory of mind about one's prey, to make predictions, to find causal relationships, and, using all the senses, to collect and interpret much data about the natural world. Persistence is important because it reflects the pursuit of valued outcomes (Mercer, 2012; See also U.S. Department of Education, Office of Educational Technology, 2013).

## MANAGING IMPULSIVITY

*The sign of intelligent people is their ability to control emotions by the application of reason.*

—Marya Mannes

Effective problem solvers have a sense of deliberativeness: They think before they act. They intentionally form a vision of a product, plan of action, goal, or a destination before they begin. They strive to clarify and understand directions, develop a strategy for approaching a problem and withhold immediate value judgments before fully understanding an idea. Reflective individuals consider alternatives and consequences of several possible directions prior to taking action. They decrease their need for trial and error by gathering information, taking time to reflect on an answer before giving it, making sure they understand directions, and listening to alternative points of view. (For additional resources on the management of impulsivity, visit managing impulsivity on Google and http://www.gigglepotz.com/hom/hom_teaching%20impulsive.pdf.)

### Managing Impulsivity and the Brain

The degree to which people are able to manage their impulsivity is dependent on two factors, one biological and one environmental.

To understand these factors, we need to look at the emotional characteristics of the human brain. The main purpose of a brain is survival, and many of the structures in the brain are involved in making certain the individual (and the species) do just that. Originally, these structures were designed to give the person the means to survive attacks from wild beasts or enemies. In contemporary society, the dangers are often not physical but social. However, the brain doesn't differentiate between the two; the same mechanisms are at play no matter what the source of real or perceived threat.

When a person perceives a situation to be threatening, a number of changes occur in the brain. Chemicals are released that increase heart rate and lung capacity, increase visual alertness, provide glucose for extra strength, and decrease all unnecessary functions such as digestion and immune function. (This biological response is commonly called the "fight, flight, or freeze" response.) All these changes put individuals on alert and increase their chances of survival. However, there is a downside to this system, and it occurs in the cortex of the brain. The cortex is where rational thinking and problem solving take place. It is also where one manages impulsivity. During a time of perceived threat, the cortex becomes less efficient. (Think about a time when you were insulted and could not think of a good retort until the next day!)

The upside of the fight-or-flight response is that after the initial reaction, we have a choice of ways to respond. For example, if while I'm hiking I see a curved shape on the path that looks somewhat like a snake, I may jump and scream. A few seconds later, I realize that it is a stick not a snake. At this point, I send a message to my brain saying, "Calm down, it's just a stick." The same thing occurs in social situations. Suppose my boss says something I don't like. My immediate internal reaction is to become angry and the fight-or-flight response is activated. But seconds later, I send a message to my brain saying, "I don't think either fight or flight is an appropriate response here." In this case, I have the ability to manage my initial impulsive reaction.

Not everyone manages impulsivity well. Examples are all around us from road rage in adults to children starting fights on the playground. What makes the difference between those who manage their impulsivity well and those that don't?

*Biological considerations.* There are neural pathways in the brain that lead from the rational cortex to the emotional center of the brain and give us some control over our reactions, allowing us in most instances to respond appropriately to situations. However, these pathways are not in place at birth, which is evident to every parent of a young child. In most cases, as the child matures, these pathways become more efficient and the child's responses become more appropriate. Full biological maturation of these pathways does not often occur until persons are in their mid-20s.

*The environment steps in to play a role as well.* The effectiveness of neural pathways is determined to a large degree by experience. If the only response to anger a child ever experiences is lashing out, then it is likely that the child's brain will become wired to lash out. If delaying gratification is not modeled or expected of children, they are unlikely to develop this very important characteristic.

An understanding of the neurological basis of emotional responses helps us better understand why some children do not manage impulsivity well. The age of the child is an important factor; however, neuroscientists tell us that the brain has amazing plasticity, and this is good news. It implies that children can—and should—be taught ways to manage their impulsive behaviors.

## GATHERING DATA THROUGH ALL SENSES

*Nothing reaches the intellect before making its appearance in the senses.*

—Latin proverb

All external information gets into the brain through the sensory pathways: gustatory, olfactory, tactile, kinesthetic, auditory, and visual. Most linguistic, cultural, and physical learning is derived from the environment by observing or taking in through the senses. To know a wine it must be drunk; to know a role it must be acted; to know a game it must be played; to know a dance it must be moved; to know a goal it must be envisioned. Those sensory pathways that are open, alert, and acute absorb more information from the environment than those pathways that are withered, immune, and oblivious to sensory stimuli do.

We gather data from internal sources as well. If we are in touch with our own emotions, we have to be in touch with the physical sensations in our body. For example, I know that I am fearful because my heart rate begins to speed up, my stomach clenches, and my hair stands on end. We sense what other people are experiencing or feeling by sensations that arise in our own bodies. All of us are like walking antennas, receiving and registering the felt experience of those around us. Some of us are better at this than others. To accurately register this kind of information requires being in touch with our emotional responses.

Forming mental images is important in mathematics and engineering; listening to classical music seems to improve spatial reasoning. Social scientists solve problems through scenarios and role playing; scientists build models; engineers use CAD-CAM; mechanics learn through hands-on experimentation; artists experiment with colors and textures. Musicians experiment by producing combinations of instrumental and vocal music.

## Gathering Data Through All the Senses and the Brain

The brain is the ultimate reductionist. It reduces the world to its elementary parts: photons of light, molecules of smell, sound waves, vibrations of touch—which send electrochemical signals to individual brain cells that store information about lines, movements, colors, smells, and other sensory inputs.

The neural basis for a disposition may be a blend of automatic responses to stimuli and actions guided by knowledge and expectation. The habit of gathering data through all the senses is one that clearly fits this paradigm. First, as long as the sensory receptors (the eyes, the ears, the skin, etc.) are in good working order, they will automatically, unconsciously, and simultaneously take in all the stimuli bombarding them at any given moment in time. However, this does not mean that the individual is consciously aware of all this information; much of it is determined to be irrelevant and is discarded. On the other hand, some of the stimuli (such as the temperature in the environment or other peripheral data) are encoded without the person giving them conscious attention.

You have probably experienced this phenomena many times. You walk from one room into another room for some purpose and then can't remember why you came in there. If you go back to the original room, you remember. The peripheral information from the first room was recorded unconsciously and provided the memory cue.

Another aspect of brain function that helps us understand why multiple sensory input is important is that the brain does not store a memory in a specific location; rather it is stored all over the cortex in a sort of neural circuit—the sound in the auditory cortex, images in the visual cortex, and so on. When you recall the memory, the brain reactivates or reconstructs the circuit in which it was stored. The more sensory modalities that were activated, the more triggers the brain has for reactivating the circuit. This suggests that concrete experiences in the classroom that activate several of the senses can enhance the recall of the information at a later time.

Dispositions are enhanced with knowledge and expectation. Providing educators with information about the way that the brain stores dispositions should result in their making more informed decisions as they plan their curriculum and instruction. Students also need to be informed so they can be made aware of the importance of attending to the multiple sensory aspects of their environment and how they can take advantage of these to increase their understanding and retention of information.

## THINKING INTERDEPENDENTLY

> *To keep your resolve, surround yourself with those who want you to succeed. The brain cannot do its job of protecting the body without contact with other people.*

> —Robert Ornstein and David Sobel
> in *The Healing Brain*

Human beings are social beings. We congregate in groups, find it therapeutic to be listened to, draw energy from one another, and seek reciprocity. In groups, we contribute our time and energy to tasks that we would quickly tire of when working alone. In fact, we have learned that one of the cruelest forms of punishment that can be inflicted on an individual is solitary confinement.

Cooperative humans realize that all of us together are more powerful, intellectually and/or physically, than any one individual. Probably the foremost disposition in the post-industrial society is the heightened ability to think in concert with others, to find ourselves increasingly more interdependent and sensitive to the needs of others. Problem solving has become so complex that no one person can go it alone. No one has access to all the data needed to make critical decisions; no one person can consider as many alternatives as several people can (Costa & O'Leary, 2013).

Working in groups requires the ability to justify ideas and to test the feasibility of solution strategies on others. It also requires the development of a willingness and openness to accept the feedback from a critical friend. Through this interaction the group and the individual continue to grow. Listening, consensus seeking, giving up an idea to work with someone else's, empathy, compassion, group leadership, knowing how to support group efforts, and altruism—all are behaviors indicative of cooperative human beings.

## Thinking Interdependently and the Brain

Go back in time to when our ancestors lived in caves or on savannas. Physical survival was a daily reality. Do you think people had a much better chance of surviving if they lived in a group or went it alone? The answer is obvious. Those people who learned to live and work together had a much higher survival rate, and survival is the main purpose of the human brain. So as with many brain functions, this interdependence and sociability became hardwired (See also, McGowan, 2013; Willis, 2013; Wolfe, 2013).

Neurological evidence for humans' dependence on one another is now beginning to be uncovered. Consider, for example, the role of endorphins and dopamine in the brain. Endorphins and dopamine are chemicals (neurotransmitters) produced by the brain that are active in the brain's reward system. In other words, the brain makes "feel good" chemicals that are released when certain behaviors increase the probability of survival. Endorphins are released during sustained, prolonged exercise, increasing the individual's chances of moving quickly out of danger. Your endorphin level also goes up during childbirth, decreasing pain and increasing the possibility of having a second child. Interestingly, endorphins and dopamine levels also rise during any pleasant social interaction. You get a pleasurable feeling when someone smiles at you or compliments you. This increases the probability of continued interaction with this person.

An important component of interdependent thinking— collaboration—is contingent communication. This is the mind's ability to deal with human differences—conflicting ideas, alternative perspectives, divergent points of view, and collective problem solving. Located in the prefrontal cortex, response flexibility enables the mind to attend and assess subtle verbal and nonverbal cues, and then to modify internal external reactions accordingly.

## APPLYING PAST KNOWLEDGE TO NEW SITUATIONS

*Making mental connections is our most crucial learning tool, the essence of human intelligence; to forge links; to go beyond the given; to see patterns, relationships.*

—Marilyn Ferguson

Human beings learn from experience. When confronted with a new and perplexing problem they will often draw forth experience from their past. They can often be heard to say, "This reminds me of . . ." or "This is just like the time when I. . . ." They explain what they are doing now in analogies with or references to previous experiences. They call on their store of knowledge and experience as sources of data to support theories to explain or processes to solve each new challenge. Furthermore, they are able to abstract meaning from one experience, carry it forth, and apply it in a new and novel situation.

### Applying Past Knowledge to New Situations and the Brain

At any one fraction of a second in time, the human brain is being bombarded simultaneously with an enormous amount of sensory stimuli. Paying *conscious* attention to all this information is literally impossible. Fortunately, the brain has a system to unconsciously filter this mass of information and keep only that which it considers relevant. The primary purpose of this filtering system is survival; therefore, our brains pay attention to novelty, loud noises, unusual movements, and social cues that signal danger. For survival, our brains must continually scan the environment to determine what is meaningful. Our species has not survived by taking in meaningless information. Unfortunately, however, much of what we ask students' brains to attend to is not considered by their brains to be meaningful or relevant.

Before we throw up our hands and say all is lost, we need to consider another aspect of brain functioning—how information is stored. It appears that the brain is the ultimate organizer and to keep track of everything it has stored, it uses a sort of filing system. Think of a semantic map or web and you have a metaphor for the way our brains store information in networks or maps of neural connections. When new information arrives, the brain attempts to find the appropriate network in which it will fit.

Here's where teachers' understanding of the brain comes into play. Because the new information (such as when to use a comma or determining the causes of a conflict) must make sense to the students, the teacher needs to help the students see where it fits, what they already have stored that can assist them in the understanding and storage of the concept. What the students already know is probably the prime determiner of whether the new information will make sense and therefore stored.

## FINDING HUMOR

*This I conceive to be the chemical function of humor: to change the character of our thought.*

—Lin Yutang

Another unique attribute of being human is our sense of humor. The positive effects of laughter on psychological functions include a drop in the pulse rate, the secretion of endorphins, and increased oxygen in the blood. It has been found to liberate creativity and provoke such higher-level thinking skills as anticipation, finding novel relationships, visual imagery, and making analogies. People who engage in the mystery of humor have the ability to perceive situations from an original and often interesting vantage point. They tend to initiate humor more often, to place greater value on having a sense of humor, to appreciate and understand others' humor, and to be verbally playful when interacting with others. Having a whimsical frame of mind, they thrive on finding incongruity and perceiving absurdities, ironies, and satire, finding discontinuities and being able to laugh at both situations and themselves.

## Finding Humor and the Brain

The scientific study of humor is a relatively new field of research, with most of the studies having been conducted in the past two decades. These studies have provided new insights into the role of humor in human development and what happens in the brain and in the body when you find something funny.

Humans in all cultures around the world are capable of finding humor. Babies will naturally find joy, smile, and giggle. The typical behavioral response to humor is laughter, but why do we laugh? What is its purpose? As we pointed out earlier, as a species, humans have had a better chance of survival if they are a member of a group than if they go it alone. Scientists believe that humor is one important way to promote social bonding. Laughter helps us establish and maintain our relationships and make our groups more cohesive. Given its value, it is not surprising to find that our brain has built-in mechanisms to reward us for laughing.

Three major brain components are involved in laughter and humor. First, the frontal lobes help us "get" the joke or perceive the humor in a situation. Second, the motor pathways in the brain move the muscles of the face that allow us to smile and laugh. The third component, the emotional pathway, is the most complex and requires a bit of background.

Deep within the brain is a group of structures commonly known as the *reward pathway* or the *pleasure center*. Composed of the *nucleus accumbens* and the *ventral tegmental area,* this pathway releases "feel good" brain chemicals (dopamine and endorphins) when we engage in activities that increase our chances of survival, such as eating or sex. Along with the emotional center of the brain, especially the *amygdala,* these structures serve the purpose of making us feel good and encouraging us to repeat whatever activity brought us such pleasure. Using brain-imaging techniques, scientists have discovered that these structures are explicitly involved in the perception of humor, and that is why it gives us pleasure.

Not only does humor give us feelings of pleasure and happiness, it also has significant ramifications for our psychological and physical health. Humor appears to be a universal coping mechanism we use when faced with stress. Cortisol, a rather caustic brain and body chemical released during highly stressful situations, is reduced when you laugh. The endorphins released during laughter have been shown to reduce feelings of pain. In addition, some early studies suggest that humor may boost the immune system. While much more research needs to be done in this area (called psychoneuroimmunlogy), if laughter could actually help us fight off infections, we'd have one more reason to help our students find humor in their lives.

## RESPONDING WITH WONDERMENT AND AWE

> *Wonder is what sets us apart from other life forms. No other species wonders about the meaning of existence or the complexity of the universe or themselves.*
>
> —Herbert W. Boyer

Humans share the capacity for personal intensity. Nobody is born without it. But many of us never learn to tap into the source of our intensity because we fail to discover what inspires it. Passion refers to the force for intensity in all of us. One's passions might be writing, gardening, acting, sports, and working with children, business, competition, and personal improvement.

Young children are naturally curious. They commune with the world around them; they reflect on the changing formations of a cloud, feel charmed by the opening of a bud, and sense the logical simplicity of mathematical order. They find beauty in a sunset, intrigue in the geometrics of a spider web, and exhilaration at the iridescence of a hummingbird's wings. They see the congruity and intricacies in the derivation of a mathematical formula, recognize the orderliness and adroitness of a chemical change, and commune with the serenity of a distant constellation.

Efficacious people have not only an "I can" attitude, but also an "I enjoy" feeling. They seek problems to solve for themselves and to submit to others. They delight in making up problems to solve on their own and request enigmas from others. They enjoy figuring things out by themselves and continue to learn throughout their lifetimes.

## Responding With Wonderment and Awe and the Brain

Every thought and action is accompanied by emotions. The center for emotions in the brain is the amygdala. It is deeply involved with threat, fear, and emotions of any kind. It engages many areas of the brain with chemicals and other physical interactions. Emotions have a huge impact on learning as the chemical secretions pass the information from cell to cell in the circuit. Where the secretions are positive, like serotonin, self-esteem rises and learning flourishes. These positive secretions tend to be short-lived in their emotional impact. On the other hand, where the secretions are negative, like cortisol, self-esteem dives and learning withers. Moreover, the negatives, like cortisol, linger sometimes for a long time—days rather than minutes. Those feel-good neurotransmitters (serotonin, endorphin, and dopamine) are released whenever we feel good about ourselves.

Wonderment, awe, inquisitiveness, intrigue, and mystery have their origins in the brain, and we have become curious about the question of what is the connection between survival and the human sense of wonderment. Most all brain functions can be explained by the human organism's need and drive for basic survival needs. This disposition, however, eludes this rationale and remains a mystery to us.

# LISTENING TO AND EMPATHIZING WITH OTHERS

*Listening is the beginning of understanding.*

*Wisdom is the reward for a lifetime of listening.*

*Let the wise listen and add to their learning and let the discerning get guidance.*

—Proverbs 1:5

Highly effective people spend an inordinate amount of time and energy listening. Some psychologists believe that the ability to listen to another person, to empathize with, and to understand their point of view is one of the highest forms of intelligent behavior. Being able to paraphrase another person's ideas, detecting indicators (cues) of their feelings or emotional states in their oral and body language (empathy), accurately expressing another person's concepts, emotions, and problems—all are indications of listening behavior (Piaget called it "overcoming ego-centrism"). They are able to see through the diverse perspectives of others. They gently attend to another person, demonstrating their understanding of and empathy for an idea or feeling by paraphrasing it accurately, building upon it, clarifying it, or giving an example of it.

To listen fully means to pay close attention to what is being said beneath the words. You listen not only to the "music," but also to the essence of the person speaking. You listen not only for what someone knows, but also for what one is trying to represent. Ears operate at the speed of sound, which is far slower than the speed of light the eyes take in. Generative listening is the art of developing deeper silences in yourself, so you can slow your mind's hearing to your ears' natural speed, and hear beneath the words to their meaning.

## Listening, Empathizing, and the Brain

Cells in your brain allow you to read another person's mind. Humans not only have the ability to judge the intentions and feelings of others, they often know what another person is thinking. This ability is called empathy. Empathy is both a cognitive process (the ability to understand another's emotional state) and an affective capacity (the ability to share another's emotional state). These abilities do not appear to be a learned trait; rather they appear to be hardwired in the brain. Why would this be? What would be its purpose? According to some neuroscientists, empathy serves two evolutionary functions: to create attachment and bonding between mother and child and later in life to create attachments between mates. Empathy could be considered to be part of the glue that holds relationships and societies together.

Psychologists and neuroscientists have been baffled by our ability to anticipate others' behaviors and empathize with their feelings. A team of researchers in Italy discovered what might be a key to solve this mystery. They identified a new type of neuron that fires when you perform a manual action and also fires when you watch someone else perform these actions. They have labeled "mirror neurons." Mirror neurons are what allow us to understand another's intentions and feelings. Mirror neurons, according to Feuerstein, are also fired in a child's brain upon hearing language as if the child were using these structures him- or herself. Children, thus, learn to imitate the language they hear as well as the actions they see (Feuerstein, Feuerstein, & Falik, 2010).

Studies suggest that the degree of toddlers' empathy depends, in part, on how sensitive their parents are to others. This would make sense given the theory on mirror neurons. Children learn a great deal by imitating what they see others do.

## SUMMARY

The intent of this chapter has been to provide neuroscientific support for dispositional teaching. While we have described each of nine dispositions separately, it should be cautioned that the brain does not draw them forth separately. Even for simple learning tasks, more than one area of the brain will be activated, and the more areas that are activated and engaged, the more learning takes place. For example, the use of all the senses can mean that there are several triggers to activate prior learning, and the more often these triggers are activated, the stronger the link becomes. Since the brain is pattern detector and past knowledge, if connected to the new learning, makes for much stronger knowledge generation. Therefore, one of the most worthwhile dispositions for students to acquire is that before starting on a new unit or study, some form of metacognitive reflection on what is already known promotes the new learning about to be undertaken.

Also of great importance is to keep in mind the brain's natural learning systems:

Tactile/physical movement—active total body participation

Social collaboration—thinking and learning interdependently

Emotion—passion for what is being done and learned. The "feel-good" neurotransmitters—serotonin, endorphin, and dopamine—are released whenever we feel good about ourselves

Cognition—mental engagement with relevant content

Metacognitive reflection—consideration and evaluation on one's own learning

We've learned more about the brain in the past few years than in all of recorded history. This research has provided revelations about the structure and function of the human brain and how the brain learns. While this research does not tell us how to teach, the better we understand neuroscientific research, we have a more solid foundation on which to base our educational decisions. As we explore dispositional teaching and learning, this research will help us understand how dispositions become established in the brain, and how to give our students the lasting gift of these productive behaviors.

Thus, the types of dispositions mentioned here may well serve as the most essential, enduring, powerful, and desirable attributes for the graduates of our educational system. They will need dispositions and learning skills far beyond current society requirements. Most of the jobs our students will be working at have, in fact, not been created yet. Indeed, our survival may depend on them.

## REFERENCES

Costa, A., & O'Leary, P. (Eds.). (2013). *The power of the social brain: Teaching, learning, and using interdependent thinking.* New York, NY: Teachers College Press.

Dunlosky, J., & Metcalf, J. (2009). *Metacognition.* Thousand Oaks, CA: Sage.

Feuerstein, R., Feuerstein, R., & Falik, L. (2010). *Beyond smarter: Mediated learning and the brain's capacity for change.* New York, NY: Teachers College Press.

Hacker, J., Dunlosky, J., & Graesser, A. (2009). *Handbook of metacogntion in education.* New York, NY: Routledge.

McGowan, P. (2013). Cooperation is what makes us human, Psychology: Where we part ways with our ape cousins. Retrieved from, http// nautil.us/Issue/1/what-makes-you-so-special/cooperation-is-what-makes-us-human

Mercer, J. (2012, November/December). The power of persistence. *The Intelligent Optimist,* pp. 40–48.

Mohan, G. (2013). No kidding: At 5 months babies start to figure it out. *The Sacramento Bee.* Sunday, April 21. Health and Science, p. A9.

U.S. Department of Education, Office of Educational Technology. (2013). *Promoting grit, tenacity, and perseverance: Critical factors for success in the 21st century.* Washington D.C.: Center for Technology in Learning, SRI International.

Willis, J. (2013). Cooperative learning: Accessing our highest human potential. In Costa, A., & O'Leary, P. (Eds.), *The power of the social brain: Teaching, learning, and using interdependent thinking.* New York, NY: Teachers College Press.

Wolfe, P. (2013). Thinking interdependently—A human survival mechanism. In Costa, A., & O'Leary, P. (Eds.), *The power of the social brain: Teaching, learning, and using interdependent thinking.* New York, NY: Teachers College Press.

# Dispositions by Intention: Mapping the Curriculum

*Dispositions to learning should be key performance indicators of the outcomes of schooling. Many teachers believe that, if achievement is enhanced, there is a ripple effect to these dispositions. However such a belief is not defensible. Such dispositions need planned interventions.*

—John Hattie (2009), *Visible Learning*

**W**alk into the Apple Store and you will see a classroom. There is a clear intention for developing engagement. People are in small groups around a table—their task? Learn as much as you possibly can about Apple products. What do you observe are the behaviors? Curiosity, questioning, problem solving, wonderment, and awe. Not certain how something works? Find an instructional coach. Still puzzled? Go to the genius bar where there are resources and experts in specific areas. Outcomes? One of the most successful businesses in the world (Triosi, 2013).

Let's consider this as an analogy for how we might design our curriculum and instruction in the classroom. Here are some principles to guide curriculum and instructional design:

- The curriculum is designed to intrigue—to raise consciousness about new ideas.
- There are challenging problems to be solved with much guidance available.
- There is an opportunity to practice.
- Collaboration is encouraged.
- Technology is integrated into the learning—it is seen as a tool for learning.
- There is an intentional design to foster dispositions such as curiosity, flexible thinking, listening with understanding and empathy, and persisting.

The nature of the tasks the students will engage with require practice in building dispositions. The design is challenging and rigorous. The focus of instruction is on making certain that students are aware of and are practicing the dispositions as they work. The specific dispositions are explicit so that the learner develops the habit of calling on them when faced with complex situations. Nothing short of practice builds dispositions, so curriculum and instruction must be designed to offer opportunities for practice. This chapter assists in minding the gap by exploring the design of the curriculum to ensure that the outcomes of what is taught, how they are taught, and how they are assessed.

## THREE CURRICULUM REFRAMES

In his book, *Know Your Values and Frame the Debate* (2004), George Lakoff states:

Frames are mental structures that shape the way we see the world. As a result, they shape the goals we seek, the plans we make, the way we act, and what counts as a good or bad outcome of our actions. To change our frames is to change all of this. Reframing *is* social change. . . . Reframing is changing the way the public sees the world. It is changing what counts as common sense. Because language activates frames, new language is required for new frames. Thinking differently requires speaking differently. (p. xv)

Curriculum attends to three major decisions: (1) What should be taught—*goals and outcomes,* (2) how to organize and teach toward those goals—*instruction,* and (3) how might we know if those goals are being achieved using these instructional strategies—*assessment.* It is apparent that if the dispositions listed in Chapter 3 are to become the new goals of education, then reframing our view of educational outcomes, instruction, and assessment will need to shift. Embracing dispositions as educational outcomes requires some curriculum reframing as we move from what we are presently teaching toward a broader, more essential form of education. Three basic reframes include the following:

## Reframe 1. From Knowing Right Answers to Knowing How to Behave When Answers Are Not Readily Apparent

> *A bird sings not because it has an answer but because it has a song.*

> —Maya Angelou, *I Know*
> *Why the Caged Bird Sings,* 1969

Schools tend to teach, assess, and reward convergent thinking and the acquisition of content with a limited range of acceptable answers. Life in the real world, however, demands multiple ways to do something well. A fundamental shift is required from valuing right answers as the purpose for learning to knowing how to behave when we *don't* know answers—knowing what to do when confronted with those paradoxical, dichotomous, enigmatic, confusing, ambiguous, discrepant, and sometimes overwhelming situations that plague our lives. An imperative mind-shift is essential—from valuing knowledge *acquisition* as an outcome to valuing knowledge *production* as an outcome. We want students to learn how to develop a critical stance with their work: inquiring, thinking flexibly, and learning from another person's perspective. The critical attribute of intelligent human beings is not only having information, but also knowing how to act on it.

By definition, a problem is any stimulus, question, task, phenomenon, or discrepancy for which the explanation is not immediately known. Thus, we are interested in focusing on student performance under those challenging conditions that demand strategic reasoning, insightfulness, perseverance, creativity, and precision to resolve a complex problem.

As our frame shifts, we will need to let go of our obsession with acquiring content knowledge as an end in itself and make room for viewing content as a vehicle for developing broader, more pervasive, and complex goals, such as the dispositions listed in Chapter 3. These *are* the subject matters of instruction (Heick, 2013). Content, selectively abandoned and judiciously selected because of its fecund contributions to the practice and development of these dispositions, becomes the vehicle to carry the processes of learning. The focus is on learning *from* the objectives instead of learning *of* the objectives.

## Reframe 2. From Transmitting Meaning to Constructing Meaning

*Learning is an engagement of the mind that changes the mind.*

—Martin Heiddeger

Meaning making is not a spectator sport. Knowledge is a constructive process rather than a finding. It is not the content stored in memory but the activity of constructing it that gets stored. Humans don't get ideas; they make ideas.

As scientists study the processes of learning they are realizing that a constructivist model of learning reflects their best understanding of the brain's natural way of making sense of the world. Constructivism holds that learning is essentially active. A person learning something new brings to that experience all of their previous knowledge and present mental patterns. Each new fact or experience is assimilated into a living web of understanding that already exists in that person's mind. As a result, learning is neither passive nor simply objective (Abbott & Ryan, 2006).

Furthermore, meaning making is not just an individual operation. The individual interacts with others to construct shared knowledge. There is a cycle of internalization of what is socially constructed as shared meaning, which is then externalized to affect the learner's social participation. Constructivist learning, therefore, is viewed as a reciprocal process in that the individual influences the group and the group influences the individual (Vygotsky, 1978).

Our perceptions of learning need to shift from educational outcomes that are primarily an individual's collections of subskills to include successful participation in socially organized activities and the development of students' identities as conscious, flexible, efficacious, and interdependent meaning makers. We must let go of having learners acquire *our* meanings and have faith in the processes of individuals' construction of their own and shared meanings through individual activity and social interaction. That's scary because the individual and the group may *not* construct the meaning we want them to: a real challenge to the basic educational framework with which most schools are comfortable.

## Reframe 3: From External Evaluation to Ongoing, Formative Self-Assessment

*Are we educating students for a life of tests or for the tests of life?*

As cited earlier, part of Lakoff's (2004) quotation included, "Frames . . . shape . . . what counts as a good or bad outcome of our actions" (p. xv). This implies a need to reframe our language, actions, and paradigms of assessment and evaluation of educational outcomes. We assess what we value and value what we assess. Evaluation of learning has been viewed as summative measures of how much content a student has retained. It is useful for grading and segregating students into ability groups. It serves real estate agents in fixing home prices in relationship to published test scores.

Since process-oriented goals cannot be assessed using product-oriented measurement techniques, our existing evaluation paradigm must shift as well. Assessment should be neither summative nor punitive. Rather, assessment is a mechanism for providing ongoing feedback to the learner and to the organization as a necessary part of the spiraling processes of continuous renewal: self-managing, self-monitoring, and self-modifying. We must constantly remind ourselves that the ultimate purpose of evaluation is to have students learn to become self-evaluative. If students graduate from our schools still dependent on others to tell them when they are adequate, good, or excellent, then we've missed the whole point of what learning is about.

Evaluation, the highest level of Bloom's Taxonomy (1956), means generating, holding in your head, and applying a set of internal and external criteria. For too long, adults alone have been practicing that skill. We need to shift that responsibility to students—to help them develop the capacity for self-authoring, self-analyzing, self-referencing, and self-modifying. We should make student self-evaluation as significant an influence as external evaluations (Costa & Kallick, 2004).

Dispositional goals, however, cannot be assessed using right-answer-oriented measurement techniques. It's time to move beyond our narrow approach to assessing the acquisition of content and collect evidence of learning beyond content knowledge. (This will be enlarged and defined in Chapter 7.)

## WHERE DO DISPOSITIONS FIT IN CURRICULUM DESIGN?

Anyone who designs, develops, or decides on curriculum (teachers, school administrators, or curriculum workers) has a series of simultaneous decisions to make. They have to decide what concepts, understandings, and principles students need to learn and in what order should students learn them? In what thinking processes do I want students to engage? What learning activities might be developed and/or implemented to have students experience and learn those concepts? And now, we are suggesting the addition of dispositions that might support the learning; which dispositions do we want students to take away from this learning experience? The concentric circles in Figure 6.1 attempt to show how all these decisions fit together.

### Decisions About Concepts and Understandings

National, state, provincial, and school district standards such as the Common Core State Standards often help with this decision. The beauty of dispositions is that they will deliver the Common Core and any other curriculum content, as it develops competent

**Figure 6.1** Where Do Dispositions Fit in the Curriculum Design?

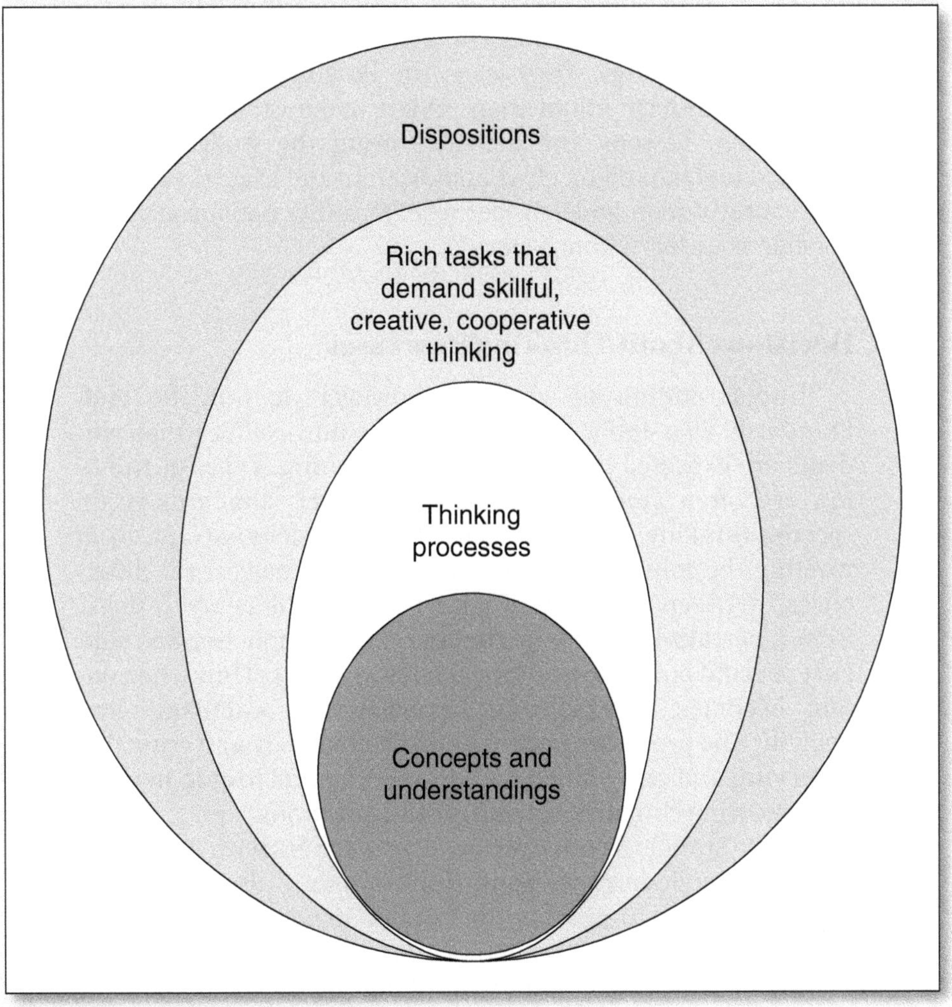

Dispositions

Rich tasks that
demand skillful,
creative, cooperative
thinking

Thinking
processes

Concepts and
understandings

lifelong learners with strategies that they can use to master any
curriculum content.

Many teachers engage in developing curriculum maps that
serve as a guide for allocating and sequencing content and skills to
be taught across grade levels and spiraling throughout the years.
Teachers often personalize the map to meet the interests, development, and current events that shape the day-to-day work in the
classroom.

For example, when studying the American Revolution, students learn some fundamental facts about the revolution. In addition, they learn about the concepts associated with a revolution as a means for change. They learn the language specific to this domain of history: minuteman, militia, colonist, sugar tax, tea party, etc.). Lessons and activities bring the students to an enlarged understanding of what indicators and triggers exist that cause a revolution and consider whether other options might be possible as we learn from history.

## Decisions About Thinking Processes

Understanding of content, however, is not the end. Standards also apply to thinking skills and *abilities* that students are expected to display in such learning. Types of thinking are often embedded in subject matter standards using specific thinking *verbs* describing what students are to do in meeting the content standard. For example, "*analyze* the differences" between two kinds of government or "*draw conclusions*" from a certain kind of experiment. *Describe* how reasons support specific points the author makes in a text. Thus, the content becomes a vehicle for experiencing, practicing, and applying the processes needed to think creatively and critically: observing and collecting data, formulating and testing hypotheses, drawing conclusions, and posing questions.

These standards not only present teachers with a pressing need to provide instruction in thinking, they also *legitimatize* taking the time to provide the kind of instruction necessary to accomplish this goal. Furthermore, they suggest that successful instruction in skillful thinking should be done *while* teaching subject matter instead of *in addition to* teaching subject matter. Thinking and subject matter content work reciprocally—you cannot learn content without giving it meaning and thinking about it; you must think about some content.

The following is an expanded list of thinking verbs that we have culled from educational standards in the Common Core and articulated by a variety of curriculum guides from states in the USA and Australia, provinces in Canada, and from other countries around the world:

Thinking Verbs Found in Curriculum Standards

| | | |
|---|---|---|
| Analyze | Diagram | Visualize |
| Apply | Identify | Reason |
| Classify | Interpret | Verify |
| Compare | Judge | Solve |
| Connect | Observe | Summarize |
| Contrast | Organize | Simplify |
| Describe | Paraphrase | Support |
| Discuss | Predict | Represent |
| Elaborate | Respond | Explore |

When these verbs are placed in context, as, for example, with the literacy standards in the Common Core, they look like this:

1. *Analyze* how and why individuals, events, and ideas develop and interact over the course of a text.

2. *Elaborate, refine, analyze,* and *evaluate* their ideas to improve and maximize creative efforts.

When we return to the example of the American Revolution, we can see how this applies.

If we unwrap those two standards in curriculum mapping, here is how the content and skills might look in a map:

Content: American Revolution—Boston Tea Party

Skills: Analyze how the Boston Tea Party started and what the effects of this were on the momentum of the revolution (cause and effect)

The standards from which the thinking words have been extracted represent a random sampling of standards included in present curricular objectives. The implication is that a student cannot demonstrate mastery of any of these required standards without performing one or more important thinking skills.

Notice how we are able to use the concentric circles (Figure 6.1) as a template for our map. We have now filled in the content (naming the specific material) and the thinking skills. Now, we can begin our assessment design.

Process outcomes, therefore, are of greater valence than the outcomes of subject-specific content because to be literate in the content, students must know and practice the processes by which that content came into being (Paul & Elder, 1994; Tishman, Perkins, & Jay, 1995). At this level, teachers answer questions such as these: What processes do I want my students to practice and develop? What thinking skills will be required to activate the mind about the big ideas I am presenting? How might I directly teach those thinking skills and processes?

## Rich Tasks That Demand Skillful, Creative, and Cooperative Thinking

Once teachers have clearly identified the content and thinking skills, they need to design the cognitive tasks that will require students to engage in deeper thinking. Many people refer to this as "backward planning" (Wiggins & McTighe, 1998). Planning from this perspective means that each level below this one will deepen students' thinking about the subject as they process material to meet the expectations of the cognitive task.

Earlier in this book, it was stated that dispositions are drawn forth in response to problems, the answers to which are not immediately known. Teachers, therefore, design rich tasks requiring strategic thinking, long-range planning, creating something new, making a decision, resolving discrepancies, clarifying ambiguities, constructing the meaning of a phenomenon, conducting research to test theories, or ameliorating polarities. If the task is not sufficiently authentic, engaging, and challenging, then students will revert to merely reproducing knowledge. When students are sufficiently challenged, they give meaning to the work, produce new knowledge, and draw on the thinking dispositions.

In the American history example, students might plan a research project to support their theories that evolutionary change need not lead to revolutionary change. Students could plan and present an exhibit demonstrating their understandings and develop rubrics for judging the exhibits and working together effectively. Additionally, they might reflect on and evaluate themselves both individually and collectively, considering how well they met criteria for the project's completion and for thinking and working interdependently.

## Deciding on Dispositions

From the broadest perspective of the curriculum landscape, students must use dispositions not only to succeed in the cognitive task that is assigned; they also learn that success is ensured by mindfully applying these dispositions. Through reflection and self-evaluation, they begin to see how the application of the dispositions transfers to all subject areas.

In the example of the American history project, students attend to communicating with accuracy and precision, persisting, and listening with understanding and empathy. As they work in their groups, they experience interdependent thinking. Finally, upon completion of the task, students reflect on the dispositions that served them in this activity. They might be asked such reflective questions as: What metacognitive strategies did you employ to manage and monitor your listening skills during your work in teams? What effect did striving for accuracy and precision have on your product? How did thinking interdependently contribute to your task accomplishment? Questions should also be posed to invite transfer to situations beyond this learning: In what other classes would it be important to strive for accuracy and precision? In what other situations beyond school would thinking interdependently contribute to your success? This attention leads to a process of internalization. Continuous explicit reference to the dispositions, practice in applying the dispositions in their work, identifying and analyzing the skills underlying each of the dispositions, and appreciating the value that the dispositions (disposition density) brings to their lives leads students to finally internalize the dispositions as a part of all that they do.

We are proposing, therefore, that teachers deliberately adopt and assess dispositions as outcomes of their curriculum and instruction. Focusing on teaching and encouraging growth in dispositional learning changes the design of their activities, determines their selection of content, and enlarges their assessments. The bigger the circle in which the outcomes live, the more influence they exert on the values of each learning (Meadows, 1997). If we wish to influence an element deeper within the system, each tiny adjustment in the environment surrounding it produces profound effects on the entire system. This realization allows us to search beyond the thinking dispositions for systems to which we naturally aspire in our journey of human development, which, if affected, also would influence our capacity to learn (Garmston, 1997).

## DEVELOPING UNITS OF WORK WITH DISPOSITIONS IN MIND

In Tahoma, Washington, Nancy Skerritt developed a collaborative model for designing curriculum that includes thinking skills, literacy, and Habits of Mind. As a result, her district has curriculum maps from K–12 that offer project-based learning in multiple disciplines, each offering the opportunity to practice deep thinking about subject matter. Here is an example of a project that focuses on the environment, climate change, and sustainability:

### Sounding Off on the Puget Sound Project

*Overview: Your job is to persuade a targeted audience to take action that will preserve and protect the Puget Sound. You will work as a member of a team and will identify a specific population for effectively communicating a message that incorporates concerns about the current state of the sound and that shares a call to action. Your goal is to influence people to make a difference in improving the Puget Sound's present and future health. Once you have identified your audience, you will want to determine what medium you will use to convey your message. Your medium may include the arts, technology, and/or speaking/writing. You are encouraged to be creative and persuasive!*

Analyze this project in light of the previous criteria:

- Intriguing? Engages curiosity?
- Collaborative?
- Encourages the use of technology?
- Fosters the need to practice dispositions?
- Requires a depth of knowledge to apply to a new context?

When we are intentionally designing for building dispositions, we need to consider the kinds of questions we might ask to make this explicit to students. For this project, we might break the questions into three categories.

### *Planning for the Project*

As you think about starting this project, describe the dispositions you think you will need to draw on.

How might the dispositions help you as you work with your team?

What commitments do you need to make with your team-mates to make certain that you will work collaboratively?

### *In Process*

What will you pay attention to as you work that will help you to determine how well you are doing?

What criteria will you use to judge the quality of your work and your process?

What has worked for you in the past?

### *After Completion of the Project*

As you anticipate future projects, what lessons have you learned from this project that you might apply?

What goals will you set for yourself as you try to become more mindful of your dispositions?

As you reflect on your work with your team, what goals might you set with your team to make certain that you are working interdependently?

## CHANGING YOUR CURRICULUM MEANS CHANGING YOUR MIND

Mapping and designing curriculum must be intentional and also responsive to the student population you are trying to serve. There must be many opportunities to practice thoughtful problem solving, creativity, and innovation and the dispositions that accompany such thinking. Michael Fullan (2012) in his book, *Stratosphere*, suggests that the work of transforming schools rests on three key elements in the stratosphere—technology, pedagogy, and change. All three need to be embedded in curriculum design. We need to make certain that we attend to, according to Vivien

Stewart's (2012) perspective, four key areas for global knowledge economies and societies:

*Science and technology-based*—requiring scientific and technological literacy

*Resource-challenged*—in need of critical thinking about sustainable economies

*Globally interdependent*—requiring global knowledge and skills as a core competence

*Innovation-driven*—placing high value on creativity and knowing how to learn

## PROVIDING THE OPPORTUNITY TO PRACTICE

If we want students to demonstrate their dispositional thinking, we need to offer them the opportunity to practice. When designing curriculum we need to consider how to offer opportunities for students to become more self-directed as they process their learning, as they aim to achieve a high level of performance. Here are some questions curriculum designers keep in mind:

Who is doing the real work? The students or the teacher?

Which dispositions are you fostering in your design?

How does the work lend itself to both the group and individuals?

What work should be done outside of the classroom and what work should be done in the classroom?

How will the students demonstrate what they have learned? Beware of too many whole class presentations.

What possibilities are there for people outside of the classroom serving as mentors or judges?

The following are a selection of many possible ways that educators are designing the opportunity to practice process as well as product:

*Create partnerships.* Bringing students to the world outside of school is often most engaging. There are many schools that offer apprenticeships in all sorts of work contexts. In addition, museums serve as an incredible resource for experiencing the world from a particular lens such as the arts or natural history. Teachers build a rich curriculum around museum visits in which the students are prepared for the visit by studying something about the exhibit that they are to see. The visit to the museum offers the opportunity for students to ask questions, develop hypotheses, imagine the possible, and, most often, see the world with wonderment and awe.

*Quests.* Schools often build curriculum designed to represent a quest, much like in gaming. Students must meet the challenges of hurdles, barriers, and a variety of complex instances as they try to make their way from one level of mastery to the next. These quests are designed to be multidisciplinary and require teamwork. See an example from the University of Maryland at: http://www.rhsmith.umd.edu/quest/whatisquest/.

*Problem-based learning.* Present students with a problem the answer to which is unknown. For example, the people in Haiti are trying to understand how to get health care into their devastated country. Without health care, they are suffering with diseases. What would you recommend is a method for making certain that when helping, you do not also make them too dependent?

*Project-based learning.* Present students with a project challenge such as the one from Tahoma Public Schools. The method that Tahoma uses is to present the project as a challenge. They then make certain that the students are connecting a real-world problem with the curriculum that they are required to teach for students to do well in the state assessments.

*Project Bright Idea.* This method of curriculum design was to bring together a cohort of teachers who would have professional development in designing curriculum for the 21st-century skills. They were trained to recognize the significance of teaching literacy, thinking skills, and Habits of Mind. Each unit is designed with that in mind. (To learn more go to Costa & Kallick, 2008, Chapter 19.)

*Flipped classroom*. Kahn Academy (http://www.khanacademy .org/) made a major contribution in demonstrating that presentations or lectures might well be recorded so that students could either listen to a podcast of the presentation or watch a video of the same. Kahn suggested that we might make a flip in which the time that is normally spent on presentation material would be accessible at home and open the time in the classroom for projects and activities that enhance the learning. As many teachers experiment with this innovative new practice, they have come to understand that technology offers new venues for learning. In essence, a flipped classroom is one in which there is a balance of virtual and face-to-face venues. This raises several questions in curriculum design: What is best learned through a presentation using technology and what is best learned through a presentation using face-to-face interaction? What is best learned through independent, self-directed work (whether at home or in school), and what requires the thoughtful interaction of the teacher and as well as significant peer interaction? As this becomes more the trend, teachers have become more aware of their need to learn how to structure a class for self-directed learning. They need to become coaches for critical and creative thinking. This curriculum design work requires team planning, communication, and problem solving so that there is a strong mix of virtual presentations that provide foundational content and skills or meaningful project-based work.

*Flipped PD*. If we expect teachers to do this work with students, they need to have a similar experience for themselves. They also need the opportunity to practice how they develop dispositional thinking as they engage with new learning. They must be able to flip the expectation that the sole source of new knowledge is the expert and discover the power of collaborative learning. Many organizations such as www.eduplanet21.com are looking at this as an approach. As teachers engage with new ideas from prominent thinkers in the field, they also engage in a social learning environment in which they construct new knowledge based on applied practice. The same criteria apply for this method as for the classroom. They learn how the venue of a video presentation feels and how they can bring a prepared mind to the various face-to-face venues in the school, such as a PLC or a department meeting. They are then able to continue their work through the social learning media. This experience requires many of the dispositions that we expect our students to be aware of, such as thinking flexibly, listening with understanding and empathy, and many others that contribute to successful collaboration and performance. As teachers learn from these methods, they are more likely to understand how to plan for their students' learning. As administrators learn from these methods, they are more likely to observe and coach teaching practices.

*Thinking routines and visible thinking.* Visible thinking (VT) developed by Project Zero researchers (Ritchhart, Church, & Morrison, 2011) is a broad and flexible framework for enriching classroom learning in the content areas while fostering students' intellectual development. The key goals of VT are to (1) deepen learners' understanding of content, (2) increase motivation for learning, (3) develop learners' thinking and learning abilities, (4) develop learners' attitudes toward thinking and learning, (5) develop learners' alertness to opportunities for thinking and learning—the dispositional side of thinking, and (6) shift the classroom culture toward a community of enthusiastically engaged thinkers and learners.

Routines exist in all classrooms; they are the patterns by which we operate and go about the job of learning and working together in a classroom environment. A routine can be thought of as any procedure, process, or pattern of action that is used repeatedly to manage and facilitate the accomplishment of specific goals or tasks. Classrooms have routines that serve to manage student behavior and interactions, to organizing the work of learning, and to establish rules for communication and discourse. Classrooms also have routines that structure the way students go about the process of learning. These learning routines can be simple structures, such as reading from a text and answering the questions at the end of the chapter, or they may be designed to promote students' thinking, such as asking students what they know, what they want to know, and what they have learned as part of a unit of study.

The core routines are a set of seven or so routines that target different types of thinking from across the modules. These routines are easy to get started with and are commonly found in Visible Thinking teachers' toolkits. Try getting started with one of these routines.

What Makes You Say That?—Interpretation with justification routine

Think–Puzzle–Explore—A routine that sets the stage for deeper inquiry

Think–Pair–Share—A routine for active reasoning and explanation

Circle of Viewpoints—A routine for exploring diverse perspectives

I used to Think . . . Now I think . . . —A routine for reflecting on how and why our thinking has changed

See–Think–Wonder—A routine for exploring works of art and other interesting things

Compass Points—A routine for examining proposition

*Philosophy for children*, sometimes abbreviated to P4C, is a movement that aims to teach reasoning and argumentative skills to children. Using a community of inquiry method, the emphasis is on a group of students inquiring together into questions with the teacher as a facilitator rather than the authoritative source of information.

In a typical inquiry, a group would be presented with a thought-provoking question or situation, such as a text, image, picture book, or video clip. Some time may be spent identifying the concepts raised by the stimulus, and then participants frame their own philosophical questions in response to the stimulus and vote for the one they wish to explore. The ensuing discussion usually takes place in a circle, with the teacher/facilitator intervening to push the thinking to a deeper level but aspiring to allow the discussion to follow the emerging interests of the group. P4C stresses nonjudgmental listening, empathy, flexibility, metacognition, management of impulse, and using clear and precise language (Jackson, 2001).

*International baccalaureate.* IB teachers want their students to be inquirers, knowledgeable, and communicators. The IB curriculum provides a perfect opportunity to learn not only the rich content but to acquire the dispositions as well. These dispositions are the ones teachers of IB want to cultivate in students so that they know how to behave intelligently when confronted with problems that they cannot immediately find the answers to. These dispositions are also linked with the IB Learner Profile and the PYP Attitudes (McGrane, 2013).

## SUMMARY

If we accept that we need to prepare students for a vastly different future than we may have known, then our understanding of the focus of education also needs to shift. This change will require a curriculum that provides individuals with the dispositions necessary to engage in lifelong learning. Simultaneously, the mindset of teachers needs to shift from the information provider to one of a catalyst, model, coach, innovator, researcher, and collaborator with the learner throughout the learning process. Furthermore, the notion of assessment needs to shift toward having students learn to value feedback, to gather data about their performance, and to become self-modifying in a journey of continuous learning.

An important element indicator, according to Yong Zhao in his book on world-class learners (2012, p. 246), is that the curriculum needs to have "Student Choice: Broad and Flexible Curriculum." This flies in the face of the more prescriptive orientation that many states and systems are taking. He suggests the following indicators as a way to assess a school's commitment to transforming practices:

- How many different courses, programs, and activities are offered?
- To what degree can students construct their courses or programs?
- To what degree can students learn from outside resources, either in the local community or through online arrangements?
- To what degree does the school provide resources such as minigrants to support student-initiated activities, such as clubs or project teams?
- To what degree can students be excused from externally imposed-upon standards and assessments with good reason?
- We would need to add, What dispositions are required for students to become the self-directed, self-assessing learners this curriculum will require?

Changing the way we approach curriculum so that it addresses the 21st-century skills requires a change in perspective. Instead of mapping just the content that we want students to know, we need to map the dispositions that represent the "soft skills"—how we would like them to be when they are both in and outside of school. Mind-shifts do not come easily, as they require letting go of old habits, old beliefs, and old traditions. There is a necessary disruption when we shift mental models. If there is not, we are probably not shifting. Growth and change are found in disequilibrium, not balance.

## REFERENCES

Abbott, J., & Ryan, T. (2006). *The unfinished revolution: Learning, human behavior, community, and political paradox.* Alexandria, VA: ASCD

Bloom, B. S. (Ed.). (1956/1984). *Taxonomy of educational objectives, the classification of educational goals—Handbook I: Cognitive Domain.* New York, NY: McKay.

Costa, A., & Kallick, B. (2004). *Strategies for self-directed learning.* Thousand Oaks: CA. Corwin.

Costa, A., & Kallick. B. (2008). *Learning and leading with Habits of Mind: 16 characteristics for success.* Alexandria, VA: ASCD.

Fullan, M. (2012). *Stratosphere: Integrating technology, pedagogy, and change knowledge.* New York, NY: Pearson.

Garmston, R. (1997, Spring). Nested levels of learning. *Journal of Staff Development, 2*(18), 66–68.

Hattie, J. (2009). *Visible Learning: A synthesis of over 800 meta-analyses relating to achievement.* London, England: Routledge.

Heick, T. (2013, March 11). Shift Learning: The 7 most powerful idea shifts in learning today. *Classroom Aid.* Retrieved from, http://classroom-aid.com/2013/03/11/the-7-powerful-idea-shifts-in-learning-today/

Jackson, T. (2001). The art and craft of "gently Socratic" inquiry. In Costa, A. (Ed.), *Developing minds: A resource book for teaching thinking.* Alexandria, VA: ASCD.

Lakoff, G. (2004). *Know your values and frame the debate.* White River Junction, VT: Chelsea Green.

McGrane, M. (2013). Tech Transformation: The future is now. What do you do when you don't know how? Retrieved from, www.maggiehosmcgrane.com/

Meadows, D. (1997, Winter). Places to intervene in a system (in increasing order of effectiveness). *Whole Earth, 79–83.*

Paul, R., & Elder, L. (1994). All content has logic: That logic is given by a disciplined mode of thinking: Part I. *Teaching Thinking and Problem Solving. 16*(5), 1–4.

Perkins, D. N. (1995). *Outsmarting IQ: The emerging science of learnable intelligence.* New York, NY: The Free Press.

Ritchhart, R., Church, M., & Morrison, K. (2011). *Making thinking visible: How to foster engagement, uncover understanding and promote independence for all learners.* San Francisco, CA: Jossey Bass.

Stewart, V. (2012). Location 1938, A world-class education: Learning from international models of excellence and innovation [electronic version]. Alexandria, VA: ASCD.

Tishman, S., Perkins, M. D., & Jay, E. (1995). *The thinking classroom.* Boston, MA: Allyn and Bacon.

Triosi, T. (2013). Our children need the schools of tomorrow today. *21st Century Leadership.* Retrieved from, smartblogs.com/education/2013/05/06/our-children-need-the-schools-of-tomorrow-today/

Vygotsky, L. (1978). *Society of mind.* Cambridge, MA: Harvard University Press.

Wiggins, G., & McTighe, J. (1998). *Understanding by design.* Alexandria, VA: ASCD.

Zhao, Y. (2012). *World class learners: Educating creative and entrepreneurial students.* Thousand Oaks, CA: Corwin.

# Observing and Assessing Growth in Dispositional Learning

*We now accept the fact that learning is a lifelong process of keeping abreast of change. And the most pressing task is to teach people how to learn.*

—Peter F. Drucker

**D**ispositions may take many years to become internalized. For most, it is a lifetime endeavor. Some are born with the inclination, others need to be taught and reminded about when to use them, and still others find it an elusive quest. Our goal is to strengthen the dispositions over time, until they are used proactively with forethought and autonomously without prompting. This requires that a person is situationally alert to cues that signal the need for the disposition, and it requires that a person possess the necessary skills to execute the dispositions and to be reflective on their effectiveness in employing those skills. Obviously this does not happen overnight, in one lesson, in one term, in one year, and maybe in one lifetime.

A first step for teachers is to create consciousness and intentionality. This means building an awareness of the dispositions, why they are important to the future of students and to their parents. Teachers need to make the case of dispositions by describing situations in which dispositions play a role in motivating learning. Over the course of a school year, teachers reveal their intentions by establishing classroom goals to increase dispositional competence. The focus of the goals is for students to become more skillful in monitoring and assessing themselves in their progress toward continuous growth and deepened competence in the dispositions.

This chapter identifies and defines eight dimensions of growth over time of thinking dispositions leading to their internalization. We also include strategies to help learners become more aware of and reflective on their performance of the dispositions and to make commitments for self-improvements.

Our experiences with assessing Habits of Mind suggest eight dimensions of growth toward internalization.

## EIGHT DIMENSIONS OF INTERNALIZATION

It is easy to think of a disposition as something that we either use or don't use, that we have or don't have. It would be more accurate to describe growth by asking the following questions:

1. *Meaning.* Does the person have a conceptual understanding of the meaning of the disposition (*persisting*, for example—what does it mean)? Can they articulate what it looks like, sounds like, and feels like? Can they give some examples and nonexamples? Can they use synonyms for the label and cite instances when they used or should have used the disposition?

2. *Capacity.* How skillfully is the disposition being used? Does the person execute the disposition with confidence, grace, and style? Do they have a range of strategies, tools, and tactics to carry out the disposition?

3. *Situational awareness.* Is the disposition being used appropriately and consistently across many diverse situations? Is the person alert to situational cues that signal when to employ and when *not* to employ the disposition?

4. *Spontaneity.* Is the disposition being used autonomously—without prompting or reminding by others? Does the motivation and inclination to use the disposition emanate from within—without seeking reward, recognition, or approval from others?

5. *Benefits.* Does the person realize the benefits and values of choosing to use the disposition? Do they predict the consequences of choosing when to use or when not to use the disposition?

6. *Reflection.* Is the person reflective on their skillfulness in using the disposition—being spectators of their behavior—making a commitment to constantly improve the performance and apply the disposition in an ever-widening set of circumstances? (This capacity is known as self-directed neuroplasticity [Rock & Schwartz, 2006, p. 8].) Does the person advocate for its use by other individuals and groups?

7. *Intentionality.* Is the disposition used consciously, proactively, and intentionally? Dispositions are not habits that are on "autopilot." Being alert to situational cues, the person consciously realizes that here is a time and situation when, for example, he needs to restrain his impulse or to listen with empathy.

8. *Action.* Thomas Edison once said, "Vision without execution is hallucination." Does the person have the will and motivation to move to action on the disposition? While a person may display the first seven dimensions, the disposition must be thoughtfully acted on, carried out, and fulfilled. In addition, the person is prepared to call the uses of the disposition for others. So in a group situation, for example, the person is willing to call on the need for listening with empathy or thinking flexibly. This is probably the most challenging of all the dimensions.

## FROM DISPOSITIONS AS NAMES AND LABELS TO INTERNALIZED THOUGHT PATTERNS

> *We know how to think, thank you. But, frankly, we're just not interested.*
>
> —Facione, Sánchez, Facione, & Gainen, 1995, p. 10

Having learned the names and meanings of several dispositions, students become aware of when they use, or should have used, particular dispositions. For example, after using profanities and pounding on the computer keyboard with his fist because he couldn't get it unfrozen, Tommy states that he "should not have been so impulsive and found an alternative, more productive way to solve the problem." While he used the correct label for the disposition, it should be noted, however, that Tommy's response was in the past tense; reactive—what he *should have done*. We want to have students employ the dispositions proactively—in the future and present tense—how they *will or are employing* the dispositions. When students use dispositions proactively, it is an indication that the disposition has become internalized.

## Internalizing Dispositions

To be successful, students must come to "own" the dispositions. So what strategies might a teacher use to cause students to internalize dispositions?

We think the following:

1. *Developing a common and consistent vocabulary throughout the culture of the school and classroom.* Names and labels of dispositions provide conceptual tools for students and staff with which they can communicate, operationalize, define, and categorize behaviors. The names are heard across all disciplines, on the playground, in the cafeteria, and at home.

2. *Repeated and frequent hearing about and focusing on the disposition over time.* "Yes, we are going to focus on listening with understanding and empathy again during our class meeting today. I know we did this during our last class meeting as well. But we agreed that listening without interrupting was difficult and you said that several times you forgot and responded impulsively without thinking. Today, let's become even more aware of our listening and pay attention to what we tell ourselves when we are tempted to interrupt."

3. *Drawing attention to and finding the disposition in many settings, in varied circumstances, contexts, and situations.*

"Besides thinking interdependently in the weight room, when and where else might it be important to think interdependently?" (See Martinez, 2009.)

4. *Discussing what the disposition means and having students generate lists of attributes and generate mental pictures of what the disposition looks like and sounds like.* "So while you are working through this problem together, what might it look like and sound like if you are communicating with clarity and precision?"

5. *Posing questions intended to engage the mind (rather than behavior).* Teachers ask many questions. Notice how behavioral questions can be transformed into questions that invite thinking.

| *Questions That Invite a Behavioral Response* | *Questions That Invite Cognitive Responses* |
|---|---|
| "Why did you do that?" | "What were you thinking when you did that?" |
| "What did the author mean when . . . ?" | "What cues were you aware of?" |
| "What are your plans for . . . ?" | "As you envision . . . ?" |
| "When will you start . . . ?" | "How will you decide when to start . . . ?" |
| "Was that a good choice?" | "What criteria did you have in mind to make that choice?" |

If teachers pose questions that deliberately engage students' cognitive processing, and let students know why the questions are being posed in this way, it is more likely that students will become aware of and engage their own mental processes. They become spectators of their own thinking.

"What was *going on in your head* when . . . ?"

"What were the *benefits?*"

"As you *evaluate the effects* of . . . ?"

"By what *criteria are you judging?*"

"What will you *be aware of* next time?"

6. *Reflecting on the use of the dispositions.* Students also become spectators of their own thinking when they are invited to monitor and make explicit the internal dialogue that accompanies the dispositions. "What goes on in your head when you think creatively?" Or, "What did you hear yourself saying inside your brain when you were tempted to talk but your job was to listen?"

7. *Establishing expectations.* Students are expected to behave in a manner consistent with the disposition, and positive, descriptive feedback (not praise) is given when it is observed. "Your persistence paid off! You stuck with it until you completed your task. You really remained focused!" (Dweck, 2006).

These are some of the powerful strategies that get the disposition inside of the brain, otherwise known as "interiorizing." (For a discussion of the research supporting these strategies, please see Leinwand and Mainardi, 2006).

## ASSESSING GROWTH OF DISPOSITIONAL LEARNING

*How much do students really love to learn, to persist?*

*To passionately attack a problem or a task?*

*To watch some of their prized ideas explode and to start anew?*

*To go beyond being merely dutiful or long-winded?*

*Let us assess such things.*

—Grant Wiggins

The purpose of assessing growth of these dispositions is to have students confront themselves and reveal to others how well they have learned to cope with adverse situations and challenging problems as well as to recognize the reasons for celebration. Traditionally, we talk about assessment and what comes to mind is what we might call "precision" measurement. We are measuring for right or wrong and, in common parlance, for mastery.

However, dispositions are never fully mastered. We just continue to learn and grow based on the contexts and demands of our experiences. The assessment of growth of dispositions requires different forms of assessment both from the design of the assessment as well as from the expectations of how the assessment data will inform our curriculum, instruction, and most important, our students' capacity to become more self-evaluative.

Earlier, in the Preface, we called attention to the gap between our current paradigm of assessing the acquisition of content and the needed new paradigm of teaching and assessing dispositions. The next section of this chapter is intended to bridge that gap and to clarify the mind-shifts needed to think about assessments of dispositions and to offer many suggestions for tools and strategies to assess growth.

## A PARADIGM SHIFT: ONGOING, FORMATIVE SELF-ASSESSMENT

*When assessment is seen as learning—for students as well as for teachers—it becomes most informative and generative for students and teachers alike.*

—Carol Ann Tomlinson (2008, p. 13)

Reflect on your experiences with testing, assessments, and evaluations when you were in school. Do you remember cramming for a midterm or final exam? Or studying for a unit quiz? Or being judged on a performance? Assessments were summative.

Do you remember losing points for minor infractions? "If you are tardy for class one more time, you'll lose 10 points." Or, "If you don't pass this course you won't get into college." Assessments could be punitive.

Do you remember how congratulatory your teachers or parents were when you scored high on your exams? And your friends cheered you—"You aced the test!" Assessments were meant to compare yourself with and to impress others.

Do you remember your fear of failure? Some parents ask their physician to prescribe psychotropic medications for their normal children to enhance academic performance (Healy, 2013). Under the provisions of the No Child left Behind Act, school districts get extra federal dollars with higher test scores that lead to school officials cheating (Honolulu Star Advertiser, 2013). Assessments can lead to a distortion of need based on results.

Dispositional growth cannot be assessed using old-fashioned, content-based assessment techniques. Growth of dispositions requires different forms of assessment than does the mastery of content. This new paradigm of assessment is built on three basic principles:

*Assessment is continuous and ongoing.* In traditional assessment designs, we waited until a project or lesson was completed to assess whether learners have acquired and retained the intended knowledge and skills. The new paradigm intends for learners to constantly monitor their performance to determine if their behavior or products meets or approaches the criteria for excellence as described in the scaffold that was generated by the group or individual.

*Formative.* Formative assessment benefits students' ongoing process of learning by generating both feedback information (from the students themselves, their products or performance, their peers, and/or the teacher/coach) *and* "feed forward" strategies that enable students with their decision making as they continually restructure their understanding/skills and to modify and build more powerful ideas and capabilities.

*Self-Assessment.* We want students to become spectators of their own growth. Building from both internal and external data sources, reflections, and observations, rich and challenging learning activities provide opportunities to build the skills of monitoring and self-assessing performance and growth of dispositions. While feedback from teachers serves as a rich data source, teachers also want students to become even more self-evaluative and metacognitive about their awareness, performance, and evaluation of their dispositions (Ferriter, 2012).

This recursive process may be described as a feedback spiral. The intent of feedback spirals is to help students self-regulate. These spirals depend on a variety of information for their success. In some cases, individuals make changes after consciously observing their own feelings, attitudes, and skills. Some spirals depend on the observations of outsiders (such as "critical friends"). Once these data are analyzed, interpreted, and internalized, individuals modify their actions to more closely achieve their desired performance goals or behaviors. Thus, learners are continually self-learning, self-renewing, and self-modifying.

Each element along the spiral is described in Figure 7.1.

• *Clarify goals and purposes.* What are the purposes for what you are doing? What beliefs or values do they reflect? What outcomes would you expect as a result of your actions?

• *Plan.* What actions would you take to achieve the desired outcomes? How would you set up an experiment to test your ideas? What evidence would you collect to help inform you about the results of your actions? What would you look for as indicators your outcomes were achieved? How will you leave the door open for other discoveries and possibilities that were not built into the original design? What process will you put in place that will help you describe what actually happened?

• *Take action/experiment.* Execute the plan.

• *Assess/gather evidence.* Implement assessment strategy.

• *Study, reflect, evaluate.* Whether this is an individual or group change, how are the results congruent with stated values? What meaning can be made of the data? Who might serve as a critical friend to coach, facilitate, or mediate your learning from this experience? What have individuals learned from this action?

• *Modify actions based on new knowledge.* What will be done differently in the future as a result of reflection and integration of new knowledge? Is this plan worth trying again?

• *Revisit and clarify goals and purposes.* Do the goals still make sense? Are they still of value, or do they need to be redefined, refocused, or refined? This element returns to the first step in the spiral: clarify goals and purposes.

## Setting a Context for Assessing the Internalization of Dispositions

To assess these dispositions, we must offer opportunities for students to show us how they work. We cannot limit what we

**Figure 7.1**   Spirals of Continuous Learning

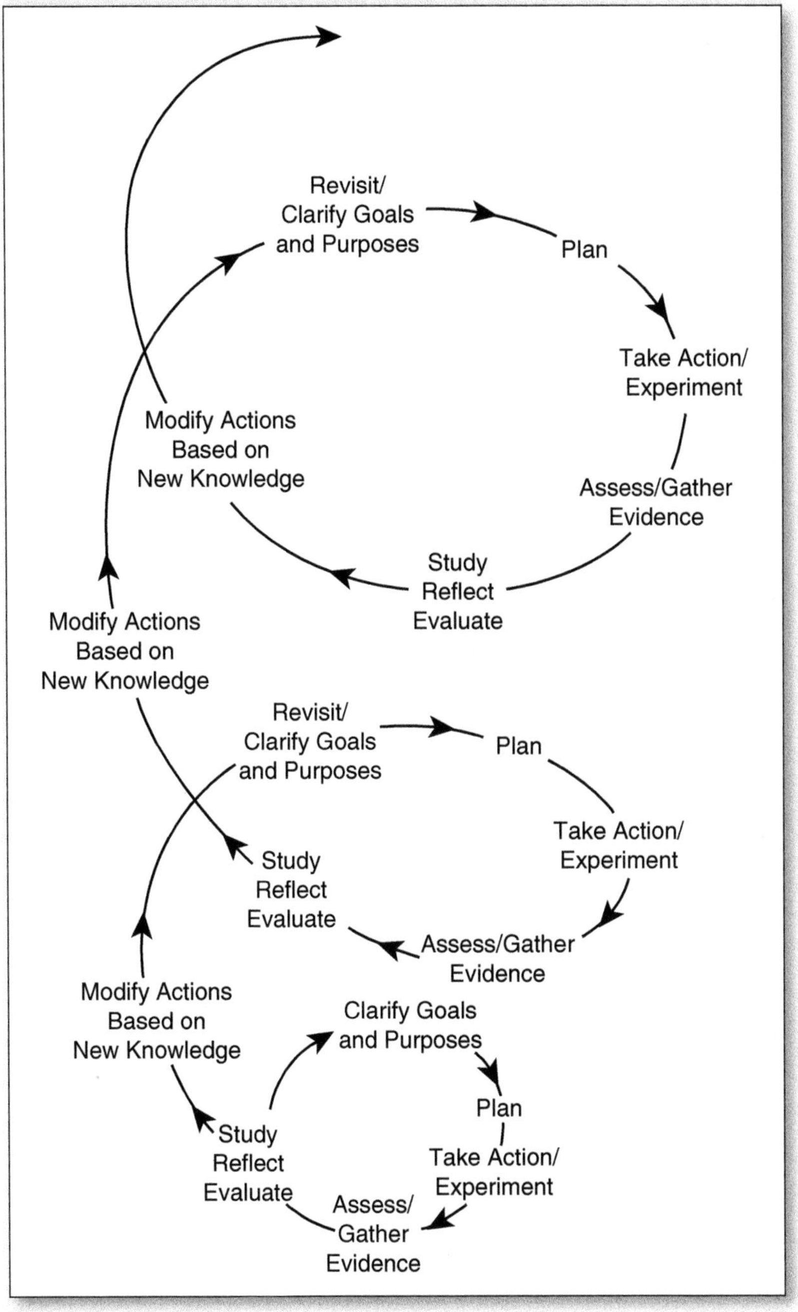

*Source:* (Costa & Kallick, 2004, p. 9)

know about a student's performance by singular measures. Davidson (2013) describes the limitations of narrowly defined assessments in this way: "Assessment is a bit like the famous Heisenberg principle in quantum mechanics: the more precisely you measure for one property, the less precisely you can measure for another. We have been spending considerable time trying to measure all levels of content knowledge with precision. In so doing, we have sacrificed recognizing and valuing the very skills that we claim to hold dear: originality, collaboration, higher-level thinking, and interdisciplinary teamwork" (p. 106). In other words, this refers to all of the so-called 21st-century skills that we identified in Chapters 2 and 3.

To make these skills measurable, we have to make them visible both to the students as well as to the teachers and parents. We need to provide many opportunities for students to show teachers, parents, peers, and themselves what they know and how skillfully they can respond when faced with a curriculum that requires thinking and problem solving. We need to be able to collect evidence of students' thinking over time so that both they and we can see the growth as they build what Ritchhart (2002) calls "intellectual character." Following are some possible ways for students to collect, reflect, and share such evidence.

In a recent document from the Office of Educational Technology of the U.S. Department of Education (2013) the authors summarized a definition of *grit* as the disposition to persist. The definition has three components that may help us to identify indicators for perseverance. The components are listed here:

1. *Academic mindsets.* These are how students frame themselves as learners, their learning environment, and their relationships to the learning environment. Mindsets include beliefs, attitudes, dispositions, values, and ways of perceiving oneself.

2. *Effortful control.* Students are constantly faced with tasks that are important for long-term goals but that in the short term may not feel desirable or intrinsically motivating. Successful students marshal willpower and regulate their attention in the face of distractions.

3. *Strategies and tactics.* Students are also more likely to persevere when they can draw on specific strategies and tactics to deal

with challenges and setbacks. They need actionable skills for taking responsibility and initiative and for being productive under conditions of uncertainty—for example, defining tasks, planning, monitoring, and dealing with specific obstacles.

Paramount to all of these considerations is the development of the student becoming more self-evaluative—being able to judge her or his own products, actions, and performances. We are aiming to move students from "I know" (awareness and meaning) to "I know I can do" (internalization and confirmation to "I can do" or to take action). Although many students use the dispositions unconsciously, it is the consciousness of the importance of these dispositions that helps them transfer the use of the dispositions to situations in which they are uncomfortable, challenged, or struggling to stay with the situation. The challenge for assessment is to make the dispositional thinking visible both to the learner and the teacher while, at the same time, aiming to make the disposition a habit—a more spontaneous use of the disposition without specific recognition.

Rick Stiggins (2012) suggests some ways of assessing growth in dispositions:

*Using the method of selected response*—designing choices that might tap into a student's awareness and feelings about the meaning and value of using particular habits given a problem or situation posed in the curriculum. For example, the student might be given the following sort of choice after a particular problem-solving assignment: On a scale from 1 to 10 (one being the lowest and 10 being the highest), how would you rate your ability to stay with the problem when it presented some difficulty for you? Explain your reasoning.

Another example: When I was working with this group I found that I was

Able to listen to the others in the group and work to understand their perspectives.

Not able to stay with the group as my mind wandered away from the task.

Interrupting people because I got frustrated with the way the group was working.

Wishing that I could do this work alone.

*Open-ended questionnaires*—in which students express their aware-ness of the meaning and value of one of the habits. For example, "As you were working on this particular problem, which of the dis-positions did you find you were calling on?" Or, "In this particular situation, you were confronted with a really complex problem in which you were asked to develop your opinion about potential solutions. What helped you to persist when you felt a struggle with the task?"

*Observations of performances*—what does it look like when a stu-dent applies a disposition? What will they be doing or saying? Asking students to self-observe, peer observe, and also have teach-ers observe to infer levels of internalization of dispositions during the process of working on a product or performance.

There are many ways that students can reveal their learn-ing to others and to themselves. Many include using digital tools that allow a student to create a museum, video, film, play, website, etc. These performances should be accompanied by questions that require the student to reflect on their develop-ment of dispositions, such as, "In what ways did the use of technology challenge your ability to think flexibly? As you con-sidered which of the tools to use, what were some of your con-siderations? When you were working with the others in your group, what were some of the strategies that you used to stay on task?"

Every educator should become skillful in developing and observing students performance of these dispositions. Collecting data about students' persisting, for example, might include the fol-lowing: persevering through disappointment and challenge in their problem solving, spending additional time, consulting oth-ers, reviewing and revising their decisions when hoped-for results have not occurred?

- Look at problems from various perspectives and be open to the influence of other ideas.
- Insist on quality performance from themselves and their peers and accept nothing less.
- Reserve their conclusions until adequate data is collected. They will develop a planned strategy for attacking their problem, and they will monitor their progress and have alternatives if their plan is not working.

- Reflect on their learning in one project; synthesize and carry forth what they have learned to make applications to future projects.

We want to foster the metacognitive process through feedback from these observations. Metacognition is the humans' ability to reflect on how effectively they are handling the problem solving. When we observe students persisting with difficult tasks, overcoming frustration, setting and achieving goals, seeking help, working with others, and monitoring and adjusting to changing circumstances while accomplishing their specific goals, we are observing the metacognitive qualities (executive functions) that are vastly more important, transferrable, lasting, and essential than recalling how to factor a polynomial.

*Interviews*—holding conversations with students about their feelings, understanding, and internalization of the dispositions. For example, we might ask primary grade students questions such as the following:

- As you recall the dispositions we have discussed this year, which ones do you think you use most?
- Why do you think it's important to use these dispositions?
- What does it look like and sound like if someone is using persistence, creativity, empathy, or craftsmanship well?
- How might you describe learning these dispositions to new students, parents, or friends?
- What questions do you have about the dispositions?

We might ask secondary grade students questions such as the following:

- As you consider the dispositions we've learned this year, which are the ones that come to mind first for you?
- Describe one or two situations in which you are using one or more of the dispositions. How do you know which dispositions would be important to use in that situation?
- What observations have you made about yourself or others in light of the dispositions?
- When you have a problem in your class, in school, or at home, what do you say to yourself that reminds you to use the dispositions?

- In what ways might you encourage others to use the dispositions to support learning?
- Given what you know about yourself as a learner, which dispositions might you describe as your strengths and stretches? What are some reasons?
- What goals are you setting for yourself regarding the dispositions as you move on toward college or a career?

In any of these situations, it is not the assessment data in and of itself that is significant. Rather, it is the ability for students to use the feedback to learn about themselves and others. These assessment strategies will foster a metacognitive capacity to reflect on how effectively the students are handling themselves as learners.

Because we are all on a continuous journey of improvement of our dispositions, dispositional learning requires continuous ongoing formative assessments. Different students are at different stages in their development of these dispositions. For numerous reasons—emotional, familial, cultural, genetic, and so on—some students are more inclined to display manifestations of these dispositions than others. Presenting students with assessment data that is generated from assessments as described previously, teachers and parents will readily determine growth in the capacities and inclinations to develop their dispositions. The From–To chart describes a continuum of typical behaviors of students as they focus on developing their capacities for self-assessment and making a commitment for growth toward internalization of several of these dispositions.

| From | To | Disposition |
|------|-----|-------------|
| Gives up quickly. Gets frustrated but lacks strategies for knowing what to do when "stuck." Displays very short attention span. | Stays with a task, remains focused through to completion. Generates and employs multiple and various problem-solving strategies. | Perseverance |
| Blurts out ideas. Jumps to conclusions. Begins work without clear goals in mind. Lashes out when emotionally flooded. | Is deliberative and goal directed. Thinks and considers alternatives before responding or acting. Reflects on actions and sets goals for improvement. | Inhibition of impulse |

| From | To | Disposition |
|------|-----|-------------|
| Ignores or interrupts others. Is unaware of other's feelings/emotions. Speaks mainly from an ego-centered point of view. | Paraphrases others' ideas. Responds with empathy. Clarifies to deepen meaning. Inquiries into ideas of mutual interest. Builds on ideas of previous speakers. | Listening with understanding and empathy |
| Is rigid in thinking unable to see others' points of view. Interprets from a narrow perspective. Refuses to change mind. Holds to one alternative. Views the world ego-centrically. | Is willing to change perceptions and conclusions with additional information. Considers others' points of view. Can examine issues both holistically and analytically. Appreciates and values others' cultures, styles, and perspectives. | Flexibility and open-mindedness |
| Follows instructions or performs tasks without wondering why they are doing what they are doing. Seldom questions themselves about their learning strategies or evaluates the efficiency of their performance. Has no idea of what to do when confronting a problem. Are often unable to explain their strategies of decision making. Lacks names for commonly used cognitive processes. | Possesses a repertoire of problem-solving strategies and approaches and can track and describe progress as they are implemented. Are conscious of beliefs, values, and actions and their effects on others. Can describe what goes on in their head when employing cognitive processes (comparing, predicting, concluding, hypothesizing, etc.). | Awareness of own thinking (Metacognition) |
| Is satisfied with disorganized, incomplete, inaccurate, and error-ridden work. | Takes pride in their accomplishments. Has a desire for accuracy as they employ various strategies to check over their work. Reviews the rules and criteria to guide their work and confirms that finished products match the criteria exactly. Knows that they can continually perfect one's craft. | Desire for craftsmanship, accuracy, and precision |

"Getting better" at a disposition means that they are increasingly improving in the eight dimensions that have been referenced earlier in this chapter.

## Portfolios

This is a digital age in which the collection of work is easier and more accessible than it has ever been in the past. Harvard University's Tony Wagner (2012, para. 12) states, "I believe the U.S. Department of Education and state education departments need to develop ways to assess essential skills with digital portfolios that follow students through school."

There are many Web 2.0 tools available for students to collect their work over time (For examples, http://msumeyers.weebly .com/student-website-examples.html) (See Farr, 2013). However, the idea of a portfolio is not to just collect the work. That might make an interesting scrapbook. Rather, it is to showcase powerful examples of work in which the student can highlight not only the product but also the process. Such reflections might be prompted by the following:

> Choose work that demonstrates your capacity to persist when you were struggling. What were some of the strategies that you employed to help you make your way toward accomplishing your goal?

> Choose work that demonstrates your best use of a time management plan. What were some of the strategies that you used to help you to keep your project moving forward?

> Choose work that demonstrates your taking a risk in your work. What did you need to do to have the courage to stay with your decisions realizing that you were innovating?

> Choose work that demonstrates you thought creatively or that you generated a novel approach to solving a problem or that you generated a new and different twist on an idea.

Figure 7.2 describes a process for developing a portfolio.

Phase 1: *Collecting*—Students collect work that has some meaning for them. They put that work in a folder. Using technology,

**Figure 7.2**   Portfolios

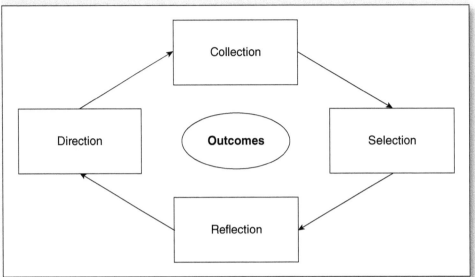

they can create a portfolio folder and then have subtitles such as: flexible thinking, using all of the senses, wonderment and awe, and craftsmanship. The teacher or the system can choose which dispositions will serve as evidence of the development of the student the school is looking for.

Phase 2: *Selection*—On a quarterly basis (or otherwise depending on the school), there is a review of the collection. At that time, students select those works that they feel are best indicators of their working on the disposition. For example, the student might choose a particular piece of writing that shows communicating with clarity and precision. Or the student might choose a video that shows how the student worked in a group and was able to work interdependently.

Phase 3: *Reflection*—The student, in each phase of this process, is developing a stronger sense of evaluation of work; it is this phase that really brings it together. The student is required to reflect on the choices made and justify the claim of how they were working on a disposition with the evidence in the working process or product.

Phase 4: *Direction*—The cycle is completed when the student takes all of the thinking and learning that has been provoked by the development of the portfolio and sets some goals for the next cycle. What do I feel really proud of? What do I think that I can improve on? What might be some benchmarks that would tell me that I am improving?

## Games

Once again, technology has pushed the frontier of using gaming for learning. Games give students immediate feedback: They might fail but they know why they've failed—the game lets them know their mistakes up front. Students can then reflect on how they may need to make modifications in their game play to be even more successful next time.

Many games require students to apply and monitor the use of such dispositions as strategic thinking, problem solving, creativity, thinking interdependently, and using clear and precise communication. If students play a multiplayer contest and win, they demonstrate that they can collaborate and strategize in teams, and the game play is designed to assess these skills. Students can be alerted to or they can discover which dispositions they must monitor and then, as they are playing the game, observers might record which dispositions are apparent and give feedback as the game play is debriefed. Teachers may want to observe students playing the games and use such checklists (as those provided here) as observational tools (Miller, 2013; Herold, 2013).

## Developing and Keeping Checklists

Invite students to describe how we can determine if they are becoming more aware of their thinking (metacognition). When asked, they can do the following:

- List the steps and tell where they are in the sequence of a problem solving strategy
- Trace the pathways and dead ends they took on the road to a problem solution
- Describe what data are lacking and their plans for producing those data

Or for persistence, they can answer the following question: What would we see or hear a person doing if they are persistent?

- Stick to it when the solution to a problem is not immediately apparent
- Employ systematic methods of analyzing a problem
- Know ways to begin, know what steps must be performed, and know when they are accurate or are in error
- Take pride in their efforts
- Strive for craftsmanship and accuracy in their products
- Become more self-directed in their problem-solving abilities
- Celebrate their achievements
- Tap into other resources (human, electronic, textual) for ideas, suggestions, and advice

Checklists are developed through conversations in the classroom. Students are asked, "What would it look like if a person were a good listener? What would it sound like if a person were a good listener?" Students generate a list of positively constructed observable behaviors. For example, in the "looks like" category, there might be responses such as, "establishes eye contact" or "nods head when agreeing." In the" sounds like" category, there might be responses such as, "builds on the other person's ideas" or "clarifies when does not understand."

The teacher then assigns or students choose a task or problem on which to work interdependently. The teacher gives directions that each student should monitor their own participation while engaging with the group to solve the problem. The students and the teacher agree to observe themselves for these behaviors.

Notice that this checklist in Figure 7.3 is titled, "How Am I Doing." A variation of this activity is to change the title of the checklist to "How Are We Doing?" The teacher invites two or three students per group (depending on the size of the group) to observe and record each group member's flexibility behavior during the task. Afterward, the teacher invites the group to reflect on their flexibility behaviors. The observer students then share the data they collected with the rest of the group. No doubt there will be dissentions and disagreements among the observers and the group members, which will provide rich learning opportunities for members of the group to listen with understanding and empathy, to communicate with precision, to metacogitate, and to manage their understanding and empathy.

Figure 7.3 is an example of a student/teacher-developed checklist for flexibility.

**Figure 7.3**   How Am I Doing Checklist

| Habit of Mind: Thinking Flexibly | OFTEN | SOMETIMES | NOT YET |
|---|---|---|---|
| Restates/paraphrases a person's idea before offering a personal opinion. | | | |
| Clarifies a person's ideas, concepts, or terminology. | | | |
| Expresses empathy for others' feelings/emotions. | | | |
| Takes an allocentric point of view, e.g., "If I were in your position" or "Looking at it from your point of view, I might . . ." | | | |
| Changes mind with addition of new information (e.g., "As a result of our discussion, I'm seeing it differently"). | | | |
| Approaches problems from different perspectives. | | | |
| Generates multiple and alternative statements of a problem. | | | |
| Displays a sense of humor. | | | |
| Laughs at oneself. | | | |

## Journals, Logs, and Diaries

Consciousness about the dispositions often begins with journal entries designed to help students focus on how they are developing. Learning logs, journals, and diaries are ways to collect evidence over time about students' self-assessment of their use of and feelings about the dispositions. They are especially powerful in engaging meta-cognition and helping students draw forth previous knowledge.

Before, or directly following, a unit, project, or area of study, invite students to make entries in their logs or journals. Short, frequent bursts of writing are sometimes more productive than infrequent, longer assignments. Teachers, too, can join in the writing process by reflecting on their teaching, analyzing learners' learning, preserving anecdotes about the class interactions, and projecting ideas for how they might approach a unit of study differently in the future.

Consider these dispositional sentence starters to help students document their learning:

- One thing that surprised me today was . . .
- I felt particularly flexible when I . . .
- I used my senses to . . .
- As I think about how I went about solving the problem, I . . .
- A question I want to pursue is . . .
- When I checked my work I found . . .
- Because I listened carefully I learned . . .

Students can collect specific log entries from time to time, read through them, and share written comments with the teacher and peers if they are so inclined. This practice helps build stronger relationships with the learners and provides a useful way for them to assess how well they are doing and how their conscious use of the Habits of Mind is developing. Initial journal entries can be compared with more recent or final ones so that students can reflect on and assess their growth over time. They can then respond to the prompt: "I used to think _____ but now I think _____."

## Rubrics

Involving students in developing and applying rubrics is another way to for them to assess their performance of dispositions. The purpose of rubrics is for self-mastery. Through student's self-authoring of descriptions and indicators of what they will be doing and saying if they are using the disposition effectively, rubrics promote self-managing, self-monitoring, and self-evaluating. They provide a mental rehearsal prior to performance. The intent is for students to describe the categories of behaviors, hold them in their head as they apply them, and then evaluate their performance and make plans for improvement (See Figure 7.1). Each category should be sufficiently clear so students can learn from the feedback about their behavior and to seek ways to improve. Following are two examples of rubrics developed by upper-grade students from Kittredge School in San Francisco under the direction of their mentor, Chuck Lavaroni. Notice that the statements begin with "I" or that they are about "me." Several statements also invite students to describe their feelings as well as their performances.

**Figure 7.4**   Student Self-Assessment Survey

*Persisting*

Directions for use:

1. Write your name, your teacher's name, and date in the appropriate spaces below.

2. Read the statement below for each category, and decide which best describes you and circle the numeral (1–5) that is in front of the statement.

3. After scoring yourself, decide on reaching a next higher statement about yourself. Make a plan for achieving it.

Name _____ Teacher _____ Date _____

*Staying on Task*

5. I am very proud of my ability to stay on task until whatever I am doing is finished and is done well.

4. I work hard at staying on what I am working on and usually complete it pretty well.

3. I am trying to get better at both working hard at finishing a task at doing it well, but it is hard for me.

2. I often get bored with finishing a task and sometimes don't think about how well it is being done.

1. I seldom finish anything; who cares anyway?

*Staying Focused*

5. Whenever I have something to do I will stay focused and not let anything get in my way as complete the task.

4. I find staying focused on what I am supposed to do is getting easier and easier. But I have to remind myself every once in a while.

3. Staying focused is hard for me, but I like it when I do it.

2. I can't stay focused unless I am really interested in what I am doing.

1. Staying focused on any one thing is very boring, so I just don't try.

*Following Through*

5. I am very pleased with my ability and willingness to follow through with anything I agree to do.

4. Following through is important to me, and I am trying to get better at it.

3. When reminded, I usually follow through with what I am expected to do.

2. I realize that I need to work harder at following through on what I am supposed to be doing.

1. Following through just doesn't work for me.

*Self-Motivation*

5. I persist because I want to; it pleases me. I do not need to have anybody encouraging me.

4. I try to take responsibility for my own persistence, but I sometimes need someone to encourage me.

3. It is hard for me to stay persisting without someone guiding or encouraging me.

2. If no one is encouraging me, I will just as well give up.

1. If "it" doesn't come easily it is not worth doing, so why persist?

**Figure 7.5**   Metacognition

*Describing*

5. I am very proud that I can and do describe what I am doing as I solve a problem, develop a new solution, or work on any thinking activity.

4. I enjoy describing the thinking I do as I solve a problem or develop some new answer, story, or solution

3. I find it difficult to describe the thinking I am doing during the time I am working on a project, solution, or new answer.

*(Continued)*

(Continued)

2. Describing what I am doing as I am thinking about what I am learning is almost impossible for me.

1. I get angry when people ask me what I am doing as I think; in fact, I refuse to think about what I am thinking while working on my learning.

*Planning*

5. I recognize how important it is to make a thinking plan or strategy before I solve a problem answer a question or create a new product.

4. I often try to develop a strategy as to what I must do to answer a question, solve a problem, or explain something new.

3. I often need help to get a strategy ready to use before I can begin a new thinking task.

2. Even with help, I find planning a thinking strategy very difficult.

1. I don't see how anyone can develop a plan or strategy for thinking; you either know it or you don't.

*Monitoring*

5. I love my ability to be able to think about or monitor my thinking as I am learning.

4. I find I do better on those occasions when I think about my learning strategy as I am learning.

3. I sometimes think about or monitor my thinking as I am involved in the work I am doing.

2. I find monitoring my thinking as I am thinking very difficult.

1. There is no way I can ever think about monitoring my thinking,

*Reflecting*

5. Thinking about or reflecting on my thinking is one of the most important skills I use because that is how I learn how to solve a problem better or develop a new solution, idea, or product.

4. When I reflect on my thinking I often get ideas that help me develop and use strategies on new issues.

3. Reflecting on my thinking is difficult but having someone help me do that makes it very interesting.

2. I find it very hard to reflect on my thinking while working, before working, or even after working on a thinking task.

1. Reflecting about my thinking is impossible and a waste of time.

(For an additional set of dispositionally related rubrics developed by the American Association for College and Universities (AACU), please email value@aacu.org.)

# USING THE POWER OF TECHNOLOGY AND SOCIAL NETWORKS

As existing knowledge becomes increasingly more accessible through the available technologies, there needs to be a shift toward paying more attention to the construction of meaning. We now realize that the input of factual information at Bloom's taxonomical (1956) levels of knowledge and comprehension are accessed more and more through technologies and less and less from textbooks and lectures. However, giving the new knowledge meaning requires building the dispositions so that students are giving meaning by asking questions such as the following:

- How do I know whether this is a credible source?
- Whose perspective is represented here? Is there another perspective I should be pursuing?
- How does my interaction with my peers influence the way I am thinking?
- Where have I learned something about this before and how does that help me to understand the meaning of this work?
- How might I create a graphic representation of this work to enhance its meaning?

Questions such as these lead students to dig more deeply into the learning. And can lead to assessment tasks that push the students to take their insights to another level and construct new knowledge through performances such as writing a play, creating a film, or building a robot. Uses of technologies offer endless possibilities for high-level performances.

Social networks increase the possibility of students sharing their work with others around the world and opens opportunities for feedback. The use of online protocols (McDonald, Zydney, Dichter, & McDonald, 2012) helps to build in the dispositions as students become online critical friends to each others' work. Through the discipline of a protocol, they learn to question thoughtfully, to listen carefully to understand the intention of the person whose work they are reviewing, and to make certain that the work is striving for accuracy and that it has taken multiple perspectives into account. In other words we are encouraging students to share their strategies for developing problem-solving dispositions.

# MEASURING AFFECTIVE RESPONSES IN THE FUTURE

New technological instruments are being developed that can provide exciting ways to assess dispositions (For a more extensive review see of these new technologies, see U.S. Department of Education Office of Educational Technology, 2013, pp. 60–63).

Interaction patterns can be explored by tracking eye moments to see where learners focus attention during problem solving. Conati and Merten (2007) used an eye-tracking device to examine metacognitive behaviors that are relevant for learning mathematical functions. The device provided information about how learners explored the stimuli, in this case the relationship between a function's graph and equation.

There are several examples in other types of digital learning environments. Conati and colleagues studied behaviors in a digital math learning environment and found that learning goals associated with self-reported conscientiousness, "learning math," and "succeeding by myself" were associated with particular interaction patterns—using a "magnifying glass" to see a number's factorization, asking advice often, and following advice often (Conati & Maclaren, 2009; Zhou & Conati, 2003). Winne and colleagues examined how a suite of study tools, *gStudy* (http://www.learningkit.sfu.ca/), can provide evidence of learning strategies. The software detects when learners create notes, which information is selected by the learner to address in the note, and how the learner classifies this information on the basis of the note template selected (Winne et al., 2006).

Examples of affective computing methods are growing. Mcquiggan, Lee, and Lester (2007) have used data-mining techniques as well as physiological response data from a biofeedback apparatus that measures blood volume, pulse, and galvanic skin response to examine student frustration in an online learning environment.

The MIT Media Lab Mood Meter (Hernandez, Hoque, & Picard, 2012) is a device that can be used to detect emotion (smiles) among groups. The Mood Meter includes a camera and a laptop. The camera captures facial expressions, and software on the laptop extracts geometric properties on faces (like distance between corner lips and eyes) to provide a smile intensity score.

It is possible to examine which parts of the brain are active during times of anxiety or stress and the effects of some interventions. Slagter, Davidson, and Lutz (2011) investigated the effects of systematic mental training and meditation to enhance cognitive control and maintain optimal levels of arousal. Motivation was found to be associated with greater activation in multiple brain regions. Moreover, studies have reported functional and structural changes in the brain and improved performance of long-term practitioners of mindfulness and concentration meditation techniques that enhance attentional focus. These initial findings are promising evidence of the brain's plasticity.

## SUMMARY

Internalization means that the chosen dispositions serve as an internal compass that guides decisions when human beings are confronted with dilemmas, enigmas, problems, conflicts, or ambiguities. These dispositions may serve as mental disciplines. When confronted with problematic situations, students, parents, and teachers might habitually employ one or more of these dispositions by *asking* themselves, not *telling* themselves (See Pink, 2010), "What is the most *intelligent thing* I can do right now?"

We are suggesting that a consciousness about the kinds of questions that students ask of themselves will lead to growth in the dispositions. As students answer such questions, they are becoming more self-evaluative. Questions such as the following can help them develop dispositions:

How can I learn from this? What are my resources? How can I draw on my past successes with problems like this? What do I already know about the problem, what resources do I have available or need to generate?

How can I approach this problem flexibly? How might I look at the situation in another way, how can I draw on my repertoire of problem solving-strategies; how can I look at this problem from a fresh perspective (lateral thinking)?

How can I illuminate this problem to make it clearer, more precise? Do I need to check my data sources? How might I break this problem into its component parts and develop a strategy for understanding and accomplishing each step?

What do I know or not know; what questions do I need to ask, what strategies are in my mind now, what am I aware of in my own beliefs, values, and goals with this problem? What feelings or emotions am I aware of that might be blocking or enhancing my progress?

The interdependent thinker might turn to others for help. They might ask how this problem affects others; how can we solve it together, and what can I learn from others that would help me become a better problem solver?

In this chapter we have shown that answering self-reflective questions, learning from the feedback and observations of others, and documenting what the student is learning using a variety of methods will make dispositions visible, measurable, and promote growth.

Because dispositions are never fully mastered, as maybe understanding content and concepts are mastered, the purposes of assessing growth in dispositions is to have students monitor themselves, confront themselves with self-generated data, and reveal to others how well they have learned to cope with adverse situations and challenging problems. It means setting goals for themselves to constantly improve their decisions and actions and making commitments to pursue those goals in future situations. It means being alert to feedback by self-observation, seeking feedback from others, and modifying their actions to become even more efficient in the execution of their dispositions. It means self-modification—building your own new neural pathways. The learner's brain sculpts itself, otherwise, neuroscientifically known as "auto-plasticity."

# REFERENCES

Bloom, B. (1956/1984). *Taxonomy of educational objectives: Book 1: Cognitive domain.* New York, NY: Longman.

Conati, C., & Merten, C. (2007). Eye-tracking for user modeling in exploratory learning environments: An empirical evaluation. *Knowledge-Based Systems, 20*(6), 557–574. doi:10.1016/j.kno sys.2007.04.010

Conati, C., & Maclaren, H. (2009). Empirically building and evaluating a probabilistic model of user affect. *User Modeling and User-Adapted Interaction, 19*(3), 267–303. doi:10.1007/s11257–009–9062–8

Costa, A., & Kallick B. (2004). *Assessment strategies for self-directed learning.* Thousand Oaks, CA: Corwin.

Davidson, C. (2013). *Now you see it: How the brain science of attention will transform the way we live, work, and learn.* New York, NY: Viking Press.

Dweck, C. (2006). *Mindset.* New York, NY: Ballantine Books.

Facione, P. A., Sánchez, C. A., Facione, N. C., & Gainen, J. (1995). The disposition toward critical thinking. *Journal of General Education, 44*(1), 1–25.

Farr, C., (2013). Educlipper launches its "virtual pinboard" for teachers & students. *Venture Beat. Entrepreneur.* Retrieved from, http://ven turebeat.com/2013/05/07/educlipper-launches-its-virtual-pin board-for-teachers-students/

Ferriter. B. (2012, May 10). Shareski's right: My students can assess themselves! *The Tempered Radical.* Retrieved from, http://blog.wil liamferriter.com/2012/05/10/selfassessment-assessment

Healy, M. (2013, March 11). Kids use ADHD drugs to succeed draws warning. *Los Angeles Times.*

Herold, B. (2013, August 7). Researchers see video games as testing, learning tools: Play used to gauge noncognitive skills. *EdWeek,* www .EdWeek.org.

*Honolulu Star Advertiser.* (2013, March 20). Dozens indicted in school cheating scandal, p. A4.

Hoque, M., Hernandez, J., & Picard, R. (2012) *Mood meter: Large-scale and long-term smile monitoring system.* ACM SIGGRAPH Emerging Technologies.

Leinwand, P., & Mainardi, C. (2006). Beyond functions strategy & leadership. *Strategy + Business.*

Martinez, M. (2009). Notes from the gym: Using Habits of Mind to develop mind and body. In Costa, A., & Kallick (Eds.), *Habits of Mind across the curriculum.* Alexandria, VA: ASCD

McDonald, J., Zydney, J., Dichter, & McDonald, E. (2012). Going *online with protocols: New tools for teaching and learning.* New York, NY: Teachers College Press.

McQuiggan, S. W., Lee, S., & Lester, J. C. (2007). Early prediction of student frustration. In Paiva, A., Prada, R., & Pickard, R. W. (Eds.), *Proceedings of the second international conference on affective computing and intelligent interactions.* Berlin, Germany.

Miller, A. (2013). Games: A model of effective assessment. *ASCD Express: Assessment That Makes Sense, 8*(17).

Pink, D. (2010, June 9). *"Can we fix it" is the right question to ask.* Retrieved from, http://www.telegraph.co.uk/finance/7839988/Can-we-fix-it-is-the-right-question-to-ask.html

Ritchhart, R. (2002). *Intellectual character: What it is, why it matters, and how to get it.* San Francisco, CA: Jossey Bass.

Rock, D., & Schwartz, J. (2006, Summer). The neuroscience of leadership. *Strategy + Business,* 43, Booz and Co. Retrieved from, http://www.strategy-business.com/article/06207?gko=6da0a

Slagter, H. A., Davidson, R. J., & Lutz, A. (2011). Mental training as a tool in the neuroscientific study of brain and cognitive plasticity. *Frontiers in Human Neuroscience,* 5(17). doi:10.3389/fnhum.2011.00017

Stiggins, R. (2012). *Student-involved classroom assessment* (3rd ed.). Boston, MA: Pearson.

Tomlinson, C. A. (2008). Learning to love assessment. *Educational Leadership,* 65(4), 8–13.

U.S. Department of Education. Office of Educational Technology. (2013). *Promoting grit, tenacity, and perseverance: Critical factors of success in the 21st Century.* Washington, D. C.: Author.

Wagner, T. (2012). Graduating all students innovation-ready. [Published Online] Retrieved from, http://www.tonywagner.com/resources/tonys-latest-ed-week-commentary-graduating-all-students-innovation-ready-now-available

Winne, P. H., Nesbit, J. C., Kumar, V., Hadwin, A. F., Lajoie, S. P., Azevedo, R., & Perry, N. E. (2006). Supporting self-regulated learning with study software: The learning it project. *Technology, Instruction, Cognition and Learning,* 3, 105–113.

Zhou, X., & Conati, C. (2003). Inferring user goals from personality and behavior in a causal model of user affect. *Proceedings of the 8th International Conference on Intelligent user. Interfaces–IUI '03,* 211. doi:10.1145/604050.604078

# CHAPTER EIGHT

# School Cultures That Support Dispositional Learning

*Concentrate all your thoughts upon the work at hand. The
sun's rays do not burn until brought to a focus.*

—Alexander Graham Bell

**M**odern society recognizes a growing need for informed,
skilled, and compassionate citizens who value truth, openness, creativity, interdependence, balance, and love as well as the
search for personal and spiritual freedom in all areas of one's life.
It is much more likely that students will learn to value, to employ,
and to advocate these dispositions if they are in an environment
that supports dispositional learning. This chapter illuminates
some of the cultural and environmental conditions in schools that
increase the probability that the dispositions will be internalized
in not only the students but the staff as well.

# BUILDING A THOUGHT-FULL ENVIRONMENT

When we say schools and classrooms must be thought-full environments, we are playing on the meaning for the word *thoughtful:* (1) to be "full of thought" and (2) to be caring and sensitive, to be "thoughtful" of others. This chapter describes some of the key environmental conditions that would be conducive to developing desired dispositions.

## Shared Vision

> *When everyone's rowing together toward the same objective, it's extremely powerful.*
>
> —Ryan Smith, CEO of Qualtrics

Senge et al. (2000; 2012) suggest that a culture is people thinking together. As individuals share meaning, they negotiate and build a culture. Over time, as groups become more skillful in employing the dispositions, the dispositions begin to pervade the value system, resulting in the changing of the norms, practices, and beliefs of the entire organization. When the norms are articulated as values and skills, teachers in such schools take collective responsibility for their own and their students' learning (Louis et al., 1996). They are no longer "my" students or "your" students; they become "our" students.

By employing the dispositions in the everyday operation of the school, the group mind illuminates issues, solves problems, makes decisions, and accommodates differences. As shared meanings grow, the group builds an atmosphere of trust in human relationships, trust in the processes of interaction, and trust throughout the organization. The common vocabulary, the agreement on the attributes of the graduates of the school, the signals in the environment, the rituals and celebration, the communications, and recognitions all facilitate the creation of a shared vision.

# A DEEPLY HELD BELIEF

In classrooms where the dispositions succeed, there is a deeply held belief that all students can continue to learn and improve.

For many years, educators and parents alike believed programs that stress thinking and dispositional learning were intended to challenge the intellectually gifted. Indeed, some thought that any child whose IQ fell below a certain score was doomed to remedial work or compensatory drill-and-practice methods. Much research, however, with hydrocephalic, Down syndrome, senile, and brain-damaged persons demonstrates that almost anyone can achieve amazing growth in intelligent behavior with proper intervention (Feuerstein, Feuerstein, & Schur, 1997).

## From Compartmentalized Subjects to Transdisciplinary Learning

There is an underlying unity—one that would encompass not just physics and chemistry, but biology, information processing, economics, political science, and every other aspect of human affairs. If this unity were real . . . it would be a way of knowing the world that made little distinction between biological science, physical science—or between either of those sciences and history or philosophy. Once, the whole intellectual fabric was seamless. And maybe it could be that way again. (George A. Cowan, President of the Santa Fe Institute quoted in Waldrop, 1992)

More than 350 years ago, Renee Descartes (1593–1650) classified knowledge into discrete compartments. He separated algebra from the study of geometry, distinguished meteorology from astronomy, and initiated the concept of hematology.

We are still operating under this obsolescent rubric. The organization of curriculum into these static compartments, while a helpful classification system for allocating time, hiring and training teachers, managing testing, purchasing textbooks, or organizing university departments, has probably produced more problems than benefits.

Organizing curriculum around the disciplines by definition discourages teachers of different departments, grade levels, and disciplines from meeting together, communicating about and finding connections and continuities among student's learning.

Certain disciplines are perceived to be of more worth than others. Through credit requirements; time allotments; allocation of resources; national, state, and local mandates; standards; testing, and the like, schools send covert messages to students and the community concerning which subjects are of greater worth. The new generation of high-stakes tests that are aligned with the Common Core State Standards focus on English Language Arts and mathematics. The arts, however, are seldom the subject of assessment. This fractionalization across departments results in incongruent goals among the different people involved.

The disciplines, as we have known them, may no longer exist. With the advent of increased technology and the pursuit of knowledge in all quarters of human endeavor, the separate disciplines are being replaced by human activities that draw on vast, generalized, and transdisciplinary bodies of knowledge and relationships applied to unique, domain-specific settings. To be an archeologist today, for example, requires employment of radar and distant satellite infrared photography as well as understanding radioactive isotopes. Professions have combined multiple disciplines into unique and ever-smaller specialties: space-biology, genetic-technology, neurochemistry, and astrohydrology. Future careers are at the intersection of various disciplines.

What distinguish the disciplines are their modes of inquiry. Each content has a logic that is defined by the thinking that produced it: its purposes, problems, information, concepts, assumptions, implications, forms of communication, technology, and its interrelationships with other disciplines. What makes a discipline a discipline is a disciplined mode of thinking (Paul & Elder, 1994). The terms biology, anthropology, psychology, and cosmology, for example, end in "*logy*" which comes from the Greek, meaning logic. Thus, bio-*logy* is the logic of the study of life forms. Psycho-*logy* is the logic of the study of the mind and so on. All areas of study are topics of interest in which something has to be reasoned out. Mathematics means being able to figure out a solution to a problem using mathematical *reasoning*. Any subject must, therefore, be understood as a mode of figuring out correct or reasonable solutions to a certain range of problems.

The disciplines deter transfer. Knowledge, as traditionally taught and tested in school subjects, often consists of a mass of knowledge-level content that is not understood deeply enough to enable a student to think critically in the subject and to seek and find relationships with other subjects. Immersion in a discipline will not necessarily produce learners who have the ability to transfer the concepts and principles of the discipline into everyday life situations. Students acquire the idea that they learn something for the purpose of passing the test, rather than accumulating wisdom and personal meaning from the content.

The separations of the disciplines produce episodic, compartmentalized, and encapsulated thinking in students. When the biology teacher says, "Today we're going to learn to spell some biological terms." Students often respond by saying, "Spelling—in biology? No way!" Biology has little meaning for physical education, which has no application to literature and has even less connection to algebra. They may be viewed as a series of subjects to be mastered rather than habituating the search for meaningful relationships and the application of knowledge beyond the context in which it was learned.

The disciplines, presented as separate organized bodies of content, may deceive students into thinking they are incapable of constructing meaning. Students frequently have been indirectly taught that they lack the means to create, construct, connect, and classify knowledge. They are taught that organized theories, generalizations, and concepts of a particular discipline of knowledge are the polished products created by expert minds far removed from them. Thus, students may think they are incapable of generating such information for themselves. While students are challenged to learn the information, the manner in which such information was created and classified often remains mysterious. All they can hope for is to acquire other peoples' meanings and answers to questions that someone else deems important.

If students are to transfer and apply their knowledge from one situation to another, to draw forth from their storehouse of knowledge and apply it in new and novel situations, the curriculum should capitalize on the natural interdependence and interrelatedness of knowledge. It is much more likely that students will learn, internalize, and transfer dispositions if they are encountered, monitored, and reflected on in a variety of settings and in repeated contexts. Therefore, dispositions must be practiced in multiple subject areas, grade levels, and encountered repeatedly throughout the school years. A shared vision transcends grade levels and subject areas. All teachers can agree on these desirable qualities. Persistence is as valued in social sciences as it is in music and physical education. Creative thinking is as basic to science as it is to literature and the arts. Striving for accuracy and precision is as important to writers as it is to chemists. Students are more likely to internalize the dispositions because they are encountered, reinforced, transferred, and revisited throughout the school, at home, and in the community.

Working together, instructional teams decide which dispositions they want their students to develop and improve and what they will do to assist the development of their students. They consider how they might work collaboratively to determine if students are internalizing the dispositions over time. They explore strategies for how they will assess student growth in the use of the dispositions. At the same time, cognizant of their own need to model the dispositions, they determine how they will work on their dispositional thinking.

What we value as educational outcomes needs to shift from a student's collections of subskills in various content areas to the development of students' identities as conscious, flexible, efficacious, and interdependent meaning-makers. We must let go of having learners acquire someone else's meanings (including ours) and have faith in the processes of individuals' construction of their own and shared meanings through individual activity and social interaction.

We need, therefore, to put together teams of teachers who have been artificially separated by departments, and to redefine their task from teaching their isolated content to instead develop multiple intellectual capacities of students. Peter Senge (1997) contends that we are all natural systems thinkers and the findings in cognitive research are compatible and supportive of the need to move from individual to collective intelligence, from disciplines to themes, from independence to relationships.

### Persist: You're in it for the long haul

> *"Excellence is an art won by training and habituation.*
> *We do not act rightly because we have virtue or excellence,*
> *but we rather have those because we have acted rightly.*
> *We are what we repeatedly do.*
> *Excellence, then, is not an act but a habit."*

> —Aristotle

As professional educators, we may be pressured for immediate, measurable results on standardized performances. This
assumes that if teachers taught academic subjects and if students were to learn and be evaluated on how well they learn
the minute subskills in each content area, they will somehow
become the kind of people we want them to be (Seiger-
Eherenberg, 1991, p. 6). Our desire is to make learning and
instruction more reflective, more complex, and more relevant
to society's and students' diverse needs and interests now and
in their future.

In many schools, educational innovations are seldom sustained. The focus continually shifts making it difficult to determine what is most important. Some educators might say, "We did
thinking last year," without realizing that thinking is central to
the authentic practices and performances they now pursue so fer-
vently. With each new intervention considerable resources of
time, energy, and money are expended on bringing teachers along
with the new practices. (Some examples are Character Education,
Common Core State Standards, AVID, T.R.I.B.E.S. *Character
Counts*, Problem/Project Based Learning, Inquiry/Socratic
Teaching, etc.) Although each of the interventions has merit, it is
a cluster of practices, mapped across the curriculum, well con-
ceived and purposefully pursued, that will lead to improved learning for students. The power of dispositions is that they transcend
any practice and, when used by both adults and students in the
school culture, they serve to ensure the necessary dispositions for
thoughtful change. Therefore, a school needs to keep the focus on
dispositions with consistency. Experience and research tells us it
takes about three to four years of well-defined instruction with
qualified teachers and carefully constructed curriculum materials
for the dispositions to become infused.

If students are to "internalize" the dispositions, they must
encounter them again and again throughout the elementary and
secondary years in every subject and in every classroom as well as
outside of school.

We want our children to develop those habits that lead them
to become lifelong learners, effective problem solvers and decision
makers, able to communicate with a diverse population, and to
understand how to live successfully in a rapidly changing, high-
tech world.

## A Rich, Responsive Environment

Students must work in a rich, responsive environment if they are to make the dispositions their own. They need access to a variety of resources that they can manipulate, experience, and observe. For example, the classroom should be filled with a variety of data sources: computers, books, almanacs, thesauri, CD-ROMs, and databases. Students should have contact with knowledgeable people in the community. Technology provides rich opportunities for students to locate information, contact others, explore theories, gather supportive data, and test ideas. Field trips are important, too, not just for their content but because they provide students opportunities to plan for and reflect on learning.

With the Internet, students need to learn to manage an overabundance of information and resources. As they move into adulthood, they will need the discipline of the dispositions to guide their higher education and their careers (Ennis, 1996).

- Trying to be well informed
- Looking for alternatives
- Seeking as much precision as the situation requires
- Reflecting on and aware of one's basic beliefs
- Being open-minded—seriously consider other points of view and be willing to consider changing one's own position
- Withholding judgment when the evidence and reasons are sufficient to do so

A rich, responsive classroom environment helps prepare them for all these experiences.

Students should be provided with many opportunities for formal and informal *feedback* about their thinking dispositions. Through teacher feedback, peer feedback, and self-feedback, students learn about their strengths and weakness of their dispositional behavior. Feedback is one of the most powerful ways a culture teaches and expresses its values, and the purpose of *feedback* is to make sure that classroom environment is one in which dispositions are supported, encouraged, and truly valued in a way that is clear to the student (Hattie, 2012).

Feedback is not praising. Carol Dweck (2007, p. 35) states,

Praising students for their intelligence, then, hands them not motivation and resilience but a fixed mindset with all its vulnerability. In contrast, effort or "process" praise (praise for engagement, perseverance, strategies, improvement, and the like) fosters hardy motivation. It tells students what they've done to be successful and what they need to do to be successful again in the future.

Nonjudgmental feedback sounds more like this:

- You really *strived for accuracy* with your report, and your improvement shows it. You read the material over several times, outlined it, and tested yourself on it. That really worked!
- You *thought flexibly* by trying all kinds of strategies on that math problem until you finally got it.
- It was a long, hard assignment, but you *persisted* and got it done. You stayed at your desk, kept up your concentration, and used strategies to keep you focused.

## SIGNALS IN THE ENVIRONMENT

*In words are seen the state of mind and character and disposition of the speaker.*

—Plutarch

If you were to walk into a school that claimed to embrace dispositional teaching, what would be unique about it? How might you tell that "something different" was going on here? The following are some indicators:

1. You'd hear staff and students spontaneously employing dispositional language in the classroom, on the playground, and in the cafeteria. They would be aware of and recognizing the dispositions in themselves and others, and making commitments to monitor, reflect on, evaluate, and improve their dispositions.

2. In classrooms you'd see and hear teachers teaching the dispositions by alerting, experiencing, illuminating, practicing,

valuing, reflecting on, and evaluating the use of selected dispositions. Students would be engaged in lessons deliberately structured and planned to include the infusion of the dispositions. Students and staff would collaboratively design assessments that guide students to self-evaluate and self-modify their skillfulness in the disposition. Students would be self-evaluating and self-modifying their skillfulness in the disposition.

3. In the school culture you'd see and hear the dispositions being recognized when they are performed and posters and slogans in the environment signaling students and staff that the dispositions are valued outcomes of the school. School staff would model, monitor, manage, and modify their use of the dispositions, both individually and in group settings. The dispositions would become the norms of the school: "the way we do things around here." The staff would be collecting and contributing longitudinal evidence of growth. The school staff would also be collecting archives of artifacts of effectiveness: a best practices in lesson designs, student artifacts, newsletters, parent reactions and responses, vignettes, success stories, and the like.

4. In the community you'd find that parents are kept informed of their student's progress in their dispositions. Parents, new to the school, would be oriented to dispositional learning and become partners in modeling, acknowledging, and supporting the dispositions at home as well as school.

Following are some practices in schools that have embraced dispositional teaching and learning. They realize that it is much more likely that students will learn, value, and practice the desired dispositions if parents and the community are supportive (Carner & Iadavia-Cox, 2012; 2013).

Parents and community members receive newspaper articles, calendars, and newsletters informing them of the school's intent and ways they can engage children's intellects.

- Mottoes, slogans, and mission statements are visible everywhere. "LINCOLN SCHOOLS ARE THOUGHT-FULL SCHOOLS" is painted on one district's delivery trucks for all to see.
- Teachers and school officials distribute bookmarks reminding the community of which thinking dispositions have become the school's goals.

**Figure 8.1** Furr High School, Houston Independent School District, Houston, Texas

Courtesy Bertie Simmons, Principal

- "THOUGHT IS TAUGHT AT HUNTINGTON BEACH HIGH" is emblazoned on that school's notepads.
- Panthers, being the school mascot, "PANTHERS 'PAWS' TO THINK" becomes the motto of the one middle school.
- Student-made posters adorn the classrooms and corridors as reminders of the dispositions that the school promotes.
- The dispositions are plainly exhibited on the walls, corridors, and stairways.

## MONITORING DISPOSITIONAL LEARNING

In schools where the dispositional learning is successful, there is a commitment to recognizing and documenting the growth of the school as a whole. School portfolios are developed in which there is a collection of artifacts representative of the practices that build the

**Figure 8.2**   Stairs by Devon Oshiro, Red Hill Elementary School, Central Oahu School District, Honolulu, Hawaii

Courtesy Teri Ushijima, Complex Area Superintendent

school culture. Children write about, illustrate, and reflect on the use of the dispositions in a shared space. This work allows them to synthesize their thoughts and actions and to translate them into symbolic form. When these artifacts are shared, there is a sense of identity with the school culture and what it represents. Students can see the differences between the work that is entered in the early years and that of the later years. It offers an aspirational perspective for the students as they progress from year to year.

They can compare any changes in those perceptions. Students can chart the processes of strategic thinking and decision making, identifying "blind alleys" and recalling successes and "tragedies" of experimentation. Often schools are called on to make presentations about their school culture. Students can develop PowerPoint presentations and videotape or audiotape recordings of projects and performances.

### Classroom Discussions

Dispositional classrooms provide ample opportunities for peer interaction about the use, effects, benefits of, and decisions about dispositions. These are interactions in which students think together, discuss their thinking with one another, and evaluate their decisions about dispositions together. The purpose is to bring the thinking disposition alive for the student by anchoring it in meaningful interpersonal interactions (Tishman & Andrade, n.d.).

Guided discussions are always a useful way for teachers to offer insight about the dispositions. Discussions also provide an opportunity for students to process their learning. Talking about situations in which dispositions were, are, or could be applied is enormously helpful as students learn more and more about the habits. Teachers can guide specific discussions of students' problem-solving processes, inviting them to share their metacognition, reveal their intentions, and examine plans for solving a problem and sharing how the disciplines are gaining meaning, application, and importance.

## ORGANIZATIONAL NORMS

When the teachers gather for a faculty meeting, they are often confronted with a challenging problem in the school. The leader starts the session by inviting the staff to consider which dispositions will best serve the group as they debate and ultimately come to consensus about the actions they will take. The group might choose *listening with understanding and empathy and questioning* and *problem posing.* They then describe what that might look like or sound like and develop a checklist to help them determine the behaviors they will attend to. They quickly develop charts that offer indicators such as making eye contact, paraphrasing what the other has said before giving their own opinion, probing, and clarifying by asking good questions. Upon completion of the meeting, the group is asked to reflect on their own and the group's performance of those dispositions and how that performance contributed to the success of the decision-making process. The group then anticipates which dispositions might be worked on both individually and as a group in future meetings of this type.

## Modeling

Imitation and emulation are the most basic forms of learning. Teachers, parents, and administrators, therefore, should provide *models* of dispositional behavior in the day-to-day operation of the school and classroom. Teachers often and easily find examples of congruent dispositional behavior in our respected leaders, heroes, and heroines. When they bring these characters to the attention of the students, they are providing opportunities to model reasoning. This structured modeling offers students a way to model reasoning for themselves, and helps students identify reasoning behavior (or the lack of it) in everyday situations.

Teachers realize the importance of their own display of desirable dispositions in the presence of learners. In the day-to-day events and when problems arise in schools, classrooms, and homes, children must see the significant adults employing the dispositions. Modeling and the explicit communication and labeling about what is being modeled and why ensures that the message is brought into students' consciousness and consideration. Teachers will want to (Goslin, 2012)

- Reflect on their behaviors and ask themselves how congruent they are with the desired behaviors they want to see in students.

- Envision the change they want, based on strong beliefs, and model behavior that advances that vision.
- Articulate or communicate verbally the values and beliefs behind the modeled behavior and the vision of change (Goslin, 2012).

The purpose of the *modeling* is to ensure that students are provided with exemplars of what thinking dispositions look like in action. Without this consistency, there is likely to be a credibility gap. As Ralph Waldo Emerson is often quoted as saying, "What you do speaks so loudly, they can't hear what you say."

## SUMMARY

*Culture is a hard thing to change. It takes a long time, but you've just got to keep repeating things and practicing what you preach.*

—Paulett Eberhart, president and
chief executive of CDI

Some of the attributes of a thought-full environment have been described. It is more likely that students will better understand, develop the capacities, and learn to value and to apply the dispositions if they are in a trustful, risk-taking, and creative classroom environment. Teachers and administrators are encouraged to monitor the climate of their school and classrooms to ensure these conditions are sustained.

## REFERENCES

Carner, L., & Iadavia-Cox, A. (2012). *Raising caring, capable kids with habits of mind.* Westport, CT: Institute for Habits of Mind .

Carner, L., & Iadavia-Cox, A. (2013). Thinking interdependently—The family as a team. In Costa, A., & O'Leary P. (Eds.), *The power of the social brain: Teaching learning and interdependent thinking.* New York, NY. Teachers College Press.

Dweck, C. (2007). The perils and promises of praise. *Educational Leadership, 65*(2), 34–39.

Ennis, R. H. (1996). *Critical thinking.* Upper Saddle River, NJ: Prentice-Hall.

Feuerstein, R., Feuerstein, R., & Schur, Y. (1997). Process as content in education of exceptional children. In Costa, A., & Liebmann, R. (Eds.), *Supporting the spirit of learning when process is content*. Thousand Oaks, CA: Corwin.

Goslin K. (2012). Is modeling enough. *Pbi Delta Kappan, 93*(7), 42–45.

Hattie, J. (2012). *Visible learning for teachers: Maximizing impact on Learning* [electronic edition] (ISBN: 978–0415690157).

Louis, K., Marks, H., & Kruse, S. (1996). Teacher's professional community in restructuring schools. *American Educational Research Journal, 33*(4), 757–798.

Paul, R., & Elder, L. (1994). All content has logic: That logic is given by a disciplined mode of Thinking: Part I. *Teaching Thinking and Problem Solving, 16*(5), 1–4.

Seiger-Eherenberg, S. (1991). Educational outcomes for a K–12 curriculum. In Costa, A. (Ed.), *Developing minds: A resource book for teaching thinking*. Alexandria, VA: Association for Supervision and Curriculum Development.

Senge, P. (1997). Foreword. In Costa, A., & Liebmann, R. (Eds.), *Envisioning process as content*. Thousand Oaks, CA: Corwin.

Senge, P., Cambron-McCabe, N., Lucas, T., Smith, B., Dutton, J., & Kleiner, A. (2000). *Schools that learn: A fifth discipline fieldbook for educators, parents, and everyone who cares about education*. New York, NY: Currency.

Senge, P., Cambron-McCabe, N., Lucas, T., Smith, B., Dutton, J., & Kleiner, A. (2012). *Schools that learn (updated and revised): A fifth discipline fieldbook for educators, parents, and everyone who cares about education*. New York, NY: Currency.

Tishman, S., & Andrade, A. (n.d.). Thinking dispositions: A review of current theories, practices, and issues. Retrieved from, http://learnweb.harvard.edu/alps/thinking/docs/dispositions.htm

Waldrop, M. M. (1992). *Complexity: The emerging science at the edge of order and chaos*. New York, NY: Touchstone.

CHAPTER NINE

# Afterthoughts and Actions

**E**arlier we said that dispositions are not just kid stuff. Recent literature in teaching, school administration, and leadership in the business world is increasingly identifying and advocating dispositions as marks of excellence. Following are just a few illustrative examples in the domain of teaching (See Dottin, Miller, & O'Brien, 2013; Dillon, 2013). Leadership journals are citing dispositions of leaders as essential to schools and businesses. As an example, Whiteley and Domaradzki (2011, p. 66) list six leadership dispositions essential to school administrators:

> One: *Thinking and acting interdependently*—promotes a positive and collaborative learning culture through shared leadership
>
> Two: *Seeking support and feedback*—creates a professional system of support and actively engages in collegial networks
>
> Three: *Metacognition and flexibility*—incorporates into practice the intrapersonal skills of planning, problem solving, and reflecting
>
> Four: *Gathering information for improvement and innovation*—uses data-based evidence to make decisions and provide formative feedback for setting direction and planning change
>
> Five: *Effective and timely individual and group communication*—develops interpersonal skills to cultivate working relationships and to mobilize individuals and groups to action that results in improvement

Six: *Commitment to continuous growth and thinking with precision*—increases cognitive understanding through self-directed professional development

Research demonstrates that when school leaders employ these types of dispositions, articulate them to parents, staff, and students and publicly learn to model them right along with members of the school community, students achieve more (Leithwood & Seashore-Lewis, 2012; Robinson, 2011).

Examples from the business world also are proliferating. Intel Corporation lists the 16 Habits of Mind as characteristics of effective thinkers (Cashman, 2013; Kohlrieser, Goldsworthy, & Coombe, 2012; Newberg, 2012)

Following is a list of dispositions for leaders (Costa & Kallick, 2008).

## Dispositional Leadership

### 1. *Perseverance*

Leaders remain focused. They have commitment to task completion and goal achievement. They never lose sight of their own and their organization's mission, vision, and purposes.

### 2. *Interaction with others*

Leaders strive to understand their colleagues. They devote enormous mental energy to comprehending and empathizing with other's thoughts and ideas.

### 3. *Inhibition of impulse*

Leaders think before they act, remaining calm, thoughtful and deliberative. Leaders often hold back before commenting, considering alternatives, and exploring the consequences of their actions.

### 4. *Flexibility*

Leaders are adaptable. They can change perspectives, generate alternatives, and consider options. They see the big picture and can analyze the parts. They are willing to acknowledge and respect others' points of view.

### 5. *Metacognition*

Leaders are aware of their thoughts, strategies, feelings, and actions and their effects on others. Leaders "talk" to themselves as they evaluate their plans, monitor their progress, and reflect on their actions, needs, and aspirations. They are spectators of their own behavior.

### 6. *Craftsmanship*

Leaders are truth-seekers. They desire exactness, fidelity, and precision. Leaders do not accept mediocrity. They seek and provide evidence for their decisions.

### 7. *Curiosity*

Leaders are questioners and problem posers. They have a need to discover and a need to test ideas. They regard problems as opportunities to grow and learn. They are more likely to ask than to tell.

### 8. *Reservoirs of knowledge*

Leaders draw on their rich experiences, access prior knowledge, and transfer knowledge beyond the situation in which it is learned. They learn from their "mistakes."

### 9. *Alertness to situational cues*

Leaders have highly tuned observational skills. They continually collect information by listening, watching, moving, touching, tasting, and smelling.

### 10. *Communication with clarity and precision*

Leaders articulate their ideas clearly in both written and oral form. They check for understanding and monitor their own clarity of terms and expressions.

### 11. *Imagination and creativity*

Leaders try to conceive problems differently, examining alternatives from many angles. They project themselves into diverse roles, use analogies, take risks, and push the boundaries of their own limits.

### 12. *Wonderment and awe*

Leaders find the world fascinating and mysterious. They are intrigued by discrepancies, compelled to mastery, and have the energy to enjoy the journey.

### 13. *Adventuresome*

Leaders are courageous adventurers as they live on the edge of their competence. They dare to take calculated risks.

14. *Humor and joy*

Leaders have such high self-esteem that they do not take themselves too seriously. They are able to laugh at themselves and with others. They are capable of playfully interpreting everyday events.

15. *Interdependence*

Leaders recognize the benefits of participation in collaborative efforts. They seek reciprocal relationships both contributing to and learning from interaction with others.

16. *Continual learners*

Leaders resist complacency about their own knowledge. They have the humility to admit their weaknesses and display a sincere desire to continue to grow and learn.

## HABITS OF HEART

*"Heartfulness"—an awareness of self and our connection with others.*

On September 11, 2001, al-Qaeda launched a series of four coordinated terrorist attacks on the United States in New York City and the Washington, D.C., area. Nineteen al-Qaeda terrorists hijacked four passenger jets and flew them in suicide attacks into targeted buildings. Two of those planes were crashed into the north and south towers of the World Trade Center in New York City. A third plane was crashed into the Pentagon and the fourth was targeted at the United States Capitol in Washington, D.C., but crashed into a field near Shanksville, Pennsylvania. On that terrible, unforgettable day, we lost many brave men and women. Almost 3,000 people died in the attacks, including all 227 civilians and 19 hijackers aboard the four planes.

Smart, knowledgeable people are often those most susceptible to thinking and acting in unethical ways. These terrorists employed many of the dispositions listed in Chapter 3. They persevered, they were goal oriented, they were creative, they thought interdependently, and they were highly organized and precise. The problem is they lacked *Habits of the Heart.*

Teaching students to think wisely should also emphasize the positive uses to which knowledge is applied. The lists of thinking dispositions were never intended to be complete or to stand alone. Their parallels are with "Habits of the Heart." Our intentions must be subjected to the humanitarian tests: Is it fair and ethical? Is it good? Is it truthful?

Is it beautiful? How might it unite and not divide? Habits of the heart receive equal valence to guide thinking dispositions. One such list follows.

We acknowledge and appreciate the thought-full contribution of Angela White, Executive Director of the Middle Years Schooling Association, and Andrew Lines of Habits of Heart Inc., Brisbane, Australia, for giving their permission to publish this list.

## HABITS OF THE HEART

(Copyright: Lines, A., & White, A., 2013, personal correspondence)

### Compassion

An understanding and empathy for the suffering of others.

*I am living compassionately when I care for all others with empathy and understanding.*

### Love

An intense feeling of deep affection.

*I am living with love when I consider what is best for others and me in my actions and words.*

### Forgiveness

A conscious, deliberate decision to release feelings of resentment or vengeance toward a person or group who has harmed you, regardless of whether they actually deserve your forgiveness.

*I am living with forgiveness when I let go of the past/ release anger and resentment.*

### Trust

Firm belief in the reliability, truth, ability, or strength of someone or something.

*I am living with trust when I have faith in those around me.*

### Acceptance

A person's assent to the reality of a situation, recognizing a process or condition (often a negative or uncomfortable situation) without attempting to change it, protest, or exit.

*I am living with acceptance when I take responsibility for who I am and my actions and acknowledge the reality of whom I am.*

### Generosity
The act of giving without judgment.

*I am living generously when I give freely without expectation or condition.*

### Openness
A tendency to accept new ideas, methods, and changes.

*I am living openly when I consider other possibilities without judgment or assumptions.*

### Patience
The capacity to accept or tolerate delay, trouble, or suffering without getting angry or upset.

*I am living with patience when I calmly allow time to pass.*

### Gratitude
The quality of being thankful and readiness to show appreciation for and to return kindness.

*I am living gratefully when I actively seek opportunities to appreciate what I have, who I am, what others have, and who they are.*

### Stillness
The state of being quiet and calm.

*I am living with stillness when I regularly take time to connect with my inner self.*

### Intuition
The ability to understand something immediately, without the need for conscious reasoning.

*I am living with intuition when I listen to/acknowledge my inner voice and feeling.*

### Presence
The state of existing within the immediate proximity in time and space.

*I am living with presence when I attend to that which is before me.*

### Truthfulness
Consistently being truthful and honest with yourself.

*I am living with truthfulness when I am honest with others and myself.*

### Courage
Reasoned perseverance in the face of fear or adversity.

*I am living with courage when I face my fears and make a stand for what I believe in.*

### Vulnerability
Exposing yourself to uncertainty, risk, and emotional exposure.

*I am living vulnerably when I have the courage to express myself despite uncertainty, risk, and emotional exposure.*

### Humility
A modest view of one's own importance.

*I am living humbly when I celebrate my own success with consideration for others.*

## ACTIONS TO BE TAKEN

*If we teach today as we taught yesterday, we rob our children of tomorrow.*

—John Dewey

Reframing society is no easy task. Peter Medawar, British/Brazilian biologist, said, "The human mind treats a new idea the same way the body treats a strange protein; it rejects it." Trying to change parents', politicians', and educators' views, behaviors, and language, even with the best possible justification, will generate discomfort. The brain sends out powerful messages that something is wrong, and the capacity for higher thought is decreased. Change itself, thus, amplifies stress and discomfort. Leaders who advocate the needed changes may not perceive them in the same way that their staff or parent community perceives them, and thus leaders tend to underestimate the challenges inherent in implementation.

So is the struggle of reframing suggested in this book futile? Are we doomed to the status quo? Not hardly. Humans are also gloriously adaptive. The human brain is amazingly modifiable (neuroplasticity). We continue to learn under proper conditions.

So, what actions should we take? Start with yourself.

> *Remember, a real decision is measured by the fact that you've taken new action. If there's no action, you haven't truly decided.*
>
> —Tony Robbins

Immerse yourself in this book and others of a like mind that are recommended throughout this book. Focus on and attend to the dispositional teaching and learning described herein. We know that the act of paying attention to a concept or idea over time creates chemical and physical change in the brain.

Cast these dispositions as outcomes for yourself and your institution. Our expectations shape our reality. Students', teachers', administrators', and parents' preconceptions have a significant impact on what they perceive to be important in life.

Become more of a continuous learner. Having the disposition of continual learning includes the humility of knowing that we don't know, which is the highest form of thinking we will ever learn. Paradoxically, unless we start off with humility we will never get anywhere. Our first step will be the crowning glory of all learning: the humility to know—and admit—when we don't know and not be afraid to find out (Costa & Kallick, 2008, p. 38).

Persist. Repeated, purposeful, and focused attention can lead to long-lasting personal change. Such attention shapes our identity over time. With enough concentrated attention, individual thoughts and acts of the mind become an intrinsic part of an individual's identity: who one is, how one perceives the world, and how one's brain works.

Think interdependently. Engage with others in discussions of these dispositions. It is more likely that minds are reframed through reciprocity and interaction with others. Pay particular attention to others who may resist or are reluctant to embrace the reframe. They are your friends as they help to sharpen and refine your advocacy.

Celebrate. Remember to recognize changes, no matter how small. It is important to keep the environment positive, healthy, and hopeful. We all need to know not only what we do not know, we also need to celebrate when we learn something new.

Become a model of the dispositions. Mahatma Gandhi said, "You must be the change you wish to see in the world." If we wish for a world that is more compassionate, more cooperative, and more thought-full, it must emanate from within each of us.

## REFERENCES

Cashman, K. (2013). The five dimensions of learning-agile leaders. *Forbes*. Retrieved from, http://www.forbes.com/sites/kevincashman/2013/04/03/the-five-dimensions-of-learning-agile-leaders/

Costa, A., & Kallick, B. (2008). *Learning and leading with Habits of Mind: 16 essential characteristics for success*. Alexandria, VA: ASCD.

Dillon, J. (2013, July 17). Teachers: Finished products or works in progress? *Smartblogs on Education*, www.smartblogs.com.

Dottin, E., Miller, L. A., & O'Brien, G. (2013). *Structuring learning environments in teacher education to elicit dispositions as habits of mind: strategies and approaches used and lessons learned*. Lanham, MD: University Press of America.

Kohlrieser, G., Goldsworthy, S., & Coombe, D. (2012). *Designing effective projects: Beliefs and attitudes habits of mind*. New York, NY: Wiley.

Leithwood, K., & Seashore-Lewis, K. (2012). *Linking leadership to student learning*. San Francisco, CA: Jossey Bass.

Medawr, P. (Unsourced). Retrieved from, http://en.wikiquote.org/wiki/Peter_Medawar.

Newberg, A. (2012, June 14). 6 exercises to strengthen compassionate leadership. Retrieved from, http://www.fastcompany.com/1840226/6-exercises-to-strengthen-Compassionateleadership.

Robinson, V. (2011). *Student centered leadership*. San Francisco, CA: Jossey Bass.

Whiteley, G., & Domaradzki, L. (2011). *School leaders' implementation field guide: Designing and supporting high-performance teams* (self-published).

# Appendices

# Appendix A

*Resources for Dispositional Teaching and Learning*

## WEBSITES AND BLOGS

Roth, Michael. Sept 8, 2012. Learning as Freedom. *New York Times*: http://www.nytimes.com/2012/09/06/opinion/john-deweys-vision-of-learning-as-freedom.html?_r=0

Ted Talks: www.ted.com

www.Eduplanet21.com

www.instituteforhabitsofmind.com

www.instituteforhabitsofmind.ning.com

www.thinkingfoundation.com

Center for Creative Learning Today and Newsletter: www.creativelearning.com

*National Center for Teaching Thinking:*

Main Office: PO Box 590607 Newton Center, MA 02459 617-965-4604; info@nctt.net; http://www.nctt.net

Madrid Office: (34)697 213 942; vbarban@nctt.net; http://www.nctt.es

P21 Blog *Connecting the 21st Century Dots: From Policy to Practice*: http://www.p21.org/tools-and-resources/p21blog

Natural Learning Research Institute: www.nlri.org

Thinking Collaborative: http://www.thinkingcollaborative.com

Tony Wagner on the seven essential skills for young people: www.youtube.com/watch?v=D3gpjjIOqHA

## RESEARCH STUDIES AND IMPLEMENTATIONS

Claxton, G. (2008). *What's the point of school? Rediscovering the heart of education*. Oxford, England: Oneworld.

Claxton, G., Chambers, M., Powell, G., & Lucas, B. (2011). *The impact of BLP: Does it work? In The learning powered school: Pioneering 21st century education*. Bristol, UK: TLO Limited.

Costa, A., & Kallick, B. (2008). Project bright idea. In *Learning and leading with habits of mind: 16 characteristics of success*. Alexandria, VA: ASCD.

Edwards, J. (2014). *A synthesis of research on habits of mind*. Mechanicsburg, PA: Institute for Habits of Mind.

Hanford, Emily. American Radio Works. Angela Duckworth and the Research on 'Grit': http/americanradioworks.publicradio.org/features/tomorrows-college/grit/angela-duckworth-grit.html

Hattie, J. (2009). *Visible learning: A synthesis of over 800 meta-analyses relating to achievement*. London, England: Routledge.

Lucas, B., Claxton, G., & Spencer, E. (2013). *Expansive education teaching learners for the real world*. Bristol, UK: TLO Limited.

Ritchhart, R. (2002). *Intellectual character: What it is, why it matters, and how to get it*. San Francisco, CA: Jossey Bass.

# INVENTORIES AND ASSESMENTS

*Assessing Personal Creativity Characteristic*. Dr. Donald J. Treffinger and Dr. Edwin C. Selby: www.creativelearning.com

Costa, A., & Kallick, B. (2008). *Learning and leading with habits of mind: 16 essential characteristics for success*. Alexandria, VA: ASCD.

Grit Scales. Psychologist Angela Duckwoth, University Pennsylvania: www.sas.upenn.edu/~duckwort/. Visit http://www.google.com/search?client=safari&rls=en&q=grit+scales&ie=UTF-8&oe=UTF-8

Kohlrieser, G., Goldsworthy, S., & Coombe, D. (2012). *Care to dare: Unleashing astonishing potential through secure leadership*. New York, NY: Wiley.

*The California Critical Thinking Dispositions Inventory*. Noreen and Peter A. Facioni. California Academic Press LLC, Jan 1, 1992 http://www.insightassessment.com/Products/Critical-Thinking-Attributes-Tests/California-Critical-Thinking-Disposition-Inventory-CCTDI

*THOMAS: The Habits of Mind Assessment Scales*: Contact Henry Toi at henrytoi@artcostacentre.com

32nd Vernon-Wall Lecture of the British Psychological Society by Prof Guy Claxton: www.bps.org.uk/search/apachesolr_search/32nd%20Vernon-Wall%20Lecture
    Powerful Learning Dispositions, p. 20
    Learning Power Questionnaire, p. 21
    Observation Schedule for Teachers and Researchers, p. 22
    Coaching Prompts, p. 23

Whiteley, G., & Domaradzki, L. (2011). *School leaders' implementation field guide: Designing and supporting high-performance teams.* Whiteley Educational.

## OTHER BOOKS BY THESE AUTHORS

Art and Bena have written and edited numerous books together and with other coauthors. Their books have been translated into Arabic, Chinese, Italian, Spanish, and Dutch. In addition to this book, their works include the following:

Costa, A. (Ed.). (2001). *Developing minds: A resource book for teaching thinking.* Alexandria, VA: ASCD.

Costa, A. (2004). *The school as a home for the mind.* Thousand Oaks, CA: Corwin.

Costa., A., & Garmston, R. (2013). *Cognitive coaching: A foundation for renaissance schools.* Lanham, MD: Rowman and Littlefield.

Costa, A., Garmston, R., & Zimmerman, D. (2014). *Cognitive capital: Assessing teacher quality.* New York, NY: Teachers College Press.

Costa, A., & Kallick, B. (1998). *Assessment in the learning organization.* Alexandria, VA: ASCD.

Costa A., & Kallick B. (2000). *Habits of Mind: A developmental series.* Alexandria, VA: ASCD.
*Discovering and exploring habits of mind*
*Activating and engaging habits of mind*
*Assessing and reporting habits of mind*
*Integrating and sustaining habits of mind*

Costa A., & Kallick, B. (2004). *Strategies for self-directed learning.* Thousand Oaks, CA: Corwin Press.

Costa A., & Kallick, B. (2009a). *Habits of Mind across the curriculum.* Alexandria, VA: ASCD.

Costa A., & Kallick, B. (2009b). *Learning and leading with Habits of Mind.* Alexandria, VA: ASCD.

Costa, A., & Liebman, R. (Eds.). (2003). *Process as content.* Thousand Oaks, CA: Corwin.
*Supporting the spirit of learning: When Process Is Content*
*The process-centered school: Sustaining a Renaissance Community*
*Envisioning process as content: Toward a Renaissance Curriculum*

Costa, A., & Lowery, L. (1989). *Techniques for teaching thinking.* Pacific Grove, CA: Midwest.

Costa, A., & O'Leary, (2013). *The power of the social brain.* New York, NY: Teachers College Press.

Kallick, B., & Colosimo, J. (2009). *Using curriculum mapping and assessment to improve student learning.* Thousand Oaks, CA: Corwin.

Swartz, R., Costa, A., Beyer, B., Kallick. B., & Reagan, R. (2007). *Thinking based learning.* New York, NY: Teachers College Press.

# Appendix B

## DECLARATION ON EDUCATION FOR LIFE

### Creating a Global Groundswell for Real Learning

1. Education should prepare all young people to deal well with the real challenges of life. It should enable them to deal with tricky situations, learn difficult things, and think clearly and ethically about what matters.

2. Schools should be models of places where students learn how to live together with civility and respect for differences and commonalities.

3. We must find the voice to speak out with a passionate understanding that schools can and must be transformed. We must not allow ourselves to remain dispirited. Rather, we must change the narrative of what education must be in the 21st century.

4. To flourish in the real world, children need more than literacy, numeracy and knowledge. They need qualities of mind such as curiosity, determination, imagination and self-control. Children who have discovered the deep pride that comes from crafting and mastering things to the very best of their ability carry their habits of careful thinking and self-discipline into the examination hall and onto the playing fields of life.

5. We must find ways to document and account for how students develop the dispositions that will give them the courage to become thoughtful citizens.

6. We must invest in teachers' ability to know their students at a deeper level, and to know what kinds of evidence of their growth will be valid and reliable. Targeted and sophisticated professional development for teachers is a vital ingredient of the development of 21st century education.

7. We must recognize the gifts of all students. Not all kids are bound for college or university—nor should they be. People whose talents and interests lie in practical and physical expertise—in making, doing, crafting and fixing things—are not less intelligent than those whose bent is for arguing, writing and calculating, and they are no less worthy of our respect and admiration. In fact, extended, practical problem-solving and project work can develop positive dispositions towards learning more effectively than academic study. Scholarship is an honorable craft—and so is fixing engines. Even in the digital age we need more skilful, ingenious mechanics than we do philosophers.

Arthur L. Costa, Granite Bay, CA
Guy Claxton, Winchester, England, UK
Bena Kallick, Westport, CT

Readers are encouraged to reproduce and widely distribute this declaration, "Creating a Groundswell for Real Learning," along with reference to this book, Costa, A., & Kallick. B. (2014). *Dispositions: Reframing teaching and learning.* Thousand Oaks, CA: Corwin. Permission is granted for the declaration only.

# Appendix C

## *21st Century Skills*

The Partnership for 21st Century Skills (http://www.p21.org) lists the following essential attributes and abilities for functioning successfully in the future.

| CRITICAL THINKING: | CREATIVE THINKING: |
|---|---|
| Analysis<br>Precision and accuracy<br>Managing complexity<br>Inductive and deductive reasoning,<br>Information development | Inventive and Intuitive<br>Thinking<br>Innovation<br>Adaptability<br>Problem-solving<br>Curiosity |
| COMMUNICATION: | COLLABORATION: |
| Professional and technical and<br>writing<br>Information development<br>Rhetoric/Persuasion<br>Confidence<br>Credibility and charisma | Small group dynamics<br>Management of outcomes<br>Networking skills<br>Interpersonal |
| RESPONSIBILTY AND LEADERSIHP: | |
| Ethics, Initiative, Persistence, Accountability, Endurance and Sustainability | |
| 21st CENTURY MODEL: | |
| Global Awareness, Financial Responsibility, Civic duty, Global Economic Principles, Information Communication, Technology Literacy, Thematic Integration | |

Partnership for 21st Century Skills. (2007). *Framework for 21st century learning.* http://www.p21.org/documents/P21_Framework_Definitions.pdf

# Index

## CORWIN

A SAGE Company

The Corwin logo—a raven striding across an open book—represents the union of courage and learning. Corwin is committed to improving education for all learners by publishing books and other professional development resources for those serving the field of PreK–12 education. By providing practical, hands-on materials, Corwin continues to carry out the promise of its motto: **"Helping Educators Do Their Work Better."**